MARK OESTREICHER
& BROOKLYN LINDSEY

99 THOUGHTS FOR JUNIOR HIGHERS

BIBLICAL TRUTHS IN BITE-SIZED PIECES

simply for students

D0423596

99 Thoughts for Junior Highers
Biblical Truths in Bite-Sized Pieces

© 2013 Mark Oestreicher and Brooklyn Lindsey

group.com
simplyyouthministry.com

Credits
Authors: Mark Oestreicher and Brooklyn Lindsey
Executive Developer: Jason Ostrander
Chief Creative Officer: Joani Schultz
Editor: Rob Cunningham
Cover Art and Production: Laura Wagner and Veronica Preston

Scripture quotations marked (NIV) are taken from the Holy Bible, New International Version®, NIV®. Copyright © 1973, 1978, 1984, 2011 by Biblica, Inc.™ Used by permission of Zondervan. All rights reserved worldwide. www.zondervan.com The "NIV" and "New International Version" are trademarks registered in the United States Patent and Trademark Office by Biblica, Inc.™

Scripture quotations from THE MESSAGE. Copyright © by Eugene H. Peterson 1993, 1994, 1995, 1996, 2000, 2001, 2002. Used by permission of NavPress Publishing Group.

ISBN 978-1-4707-1028-6

10 9 8 7 6 5 4 3 2 1   20 19 18 17 16 15 14 13

Printed in the United States of America.

WHAT'S IN THIS BOOK?

READ THIS FIRST

Junior highers are amazing. Really. We think so, and we're completely confident that God thinks so.

But let's be honest: Being a junior higher can be super confusing, wildly uneven, and as frustrating as a pop quiz.

We want to help. That's why we wrote these 99 thoughts—a collection of short, honest, and right-to-the-point ideas and advice to help you out in every area of your life.

You can read all 99 of them in order. Or you can jump around and read whatever interests you. There's no right or wrong way to read this book. Well, actually, reading the book while you're wearing a bathing suit made of bacon, and underwater in a tank of sharks—that would be a wrong way to read this book. Besides, the pages aren't waterproof—duh.

You'll also notice, sooner or later, that in addition to the 99 thoughts, each chapter ends with a story from one of us (Marko or Brooklyn) as junior highers. These are completely real and true stories that happened to us and reflect what we remember thinking and feeling. But we wrote them as if we were still in junior high (even though, we're *not* in junior high anymore—that would be *really weird* if we were).

Allow us to introduce ourselves:

My name is Marko. Actually, it's Mark, and my last name starts with an O (it's that weird-looking name on the book cover); but everyone, even my mom, calls me Marko. It's just easier. I'll be honest—I'm kind of old. In fact, I'm probably older than your parents. But I still completely love hanging out with junior highers. And I get to do that all the time, since my work involves doing just that and helping other people learn about you. I live in San Diego, California, which is every bit as wonderful as it might sound. My wife and I have two kids—one of 'em, the girl, is 19 and in college; and one of 'em, the guy, is 15 and a sophomore in high school. And I have a ridiculous beard. Really. It's massive. It even has its own Twitter® account.

Hello. I'm Brooklyn. If you're reading this, then you're one of my favorite people on Earth: a junior high-age person—winner! You have no idea how much I would like to meet you. If we could hang out tomorrow and chat about your life, I'd love it. But since we may not be able to do that right away, we can hang out together in this book. I live in Florida right now, with my ridiculously wonderful husband and adorable little girls. And we also have hundreds of adopted teenagers who we care for big-time—our youth group! Consider yourself an honorary member. I hope the words you find here are helpful and fun to read. You've got a lot of potential and we'd love to see you reach it!

As you read, if you have questions or need anything, let us know. We'd love to connect with you, pray for you, and be your biggest cheerleaders.

Are you ready to read and think and pray and be encouraged? We sure hope so. Let's do this thing.

Marko and Brooklyn

99 THOUGHTS FOR JUNIOR HIGHERS

WHO AM I?

UNDERSTANDING YOURSELF

This is a good place to start, and not only because it's near the beginning of the book. You're in an awesome and semi-crazy time of life, when you're on the road to figuring out who you are, what you like, and who you want to become.

YOU'RE ONE OF A KIND

You've probably heard this before. "You're special!" "There's only one you!"

But as cheesy as those statements might sound to you, they express something both important and true: God didn't make thousands of you, or hundreds, or even two (even if you're a twin!). No other person in history has your exact genetic makeup, no other person has the physical stuff that makes you, you.

But at a deeper level, there never has been and never will be another person with the same combination of skills, interests, personality quirks, and experiences. Only you.

That's an amazing reality, and one that says something about how much God is into you. God *loves* your uniqueness.

Being unique also has a sense of potential and potency to it: *No one else* can leave a mark on the world like you can; no one else can create the same beauty (or evil) that you can create. And when you grow to understand your uniqueness more, you can learn to embrace that. You can make the choice to be your own one-of-a-kind self.

THOUGHT #2

YOU'RE MADE IN GOD'S IMAGE

When God was inventing everything in the world, he did something wild and massively gorgeous: He chose to make humans "in his own image."

Think of it like this: Imagine being an expert in robotics. One day you unveil a robot like no one has ever seen. In fact, the entire scientific world is blown away by your robot, because it can think for itself and is amazingly human-like in the ways it acts, feels, and responds. And as people start to interact with your robot, they realize something else: It's very much like *you*. It's not that the robot necessarily *looks like you*, but there's something about the robot's *character* that constantly makes people think of you—almost like they're interacting with you when they're actually interacting with your robot.

It would be fair to say that you made your robot "in your own image."

But you're not a robot made by God. You're much more than a robot!

And because you're made in the image of God (not accidentally, by the way—this was God's plan), you have human-sized portions of God's abilities and character in you.

YOU ARE KNOWN

Junior high can be a lonely time. You might even have a bunch of friends but still feel lonely from time to time.

And as you start to get to know yourself better, it's pretty normal to sometimes wonder if anyone else really knows you. Your friends might do things that make you wonder this. Even your parents might sometimes treat you in a way that makes you feel like they don't know you.

But have confidence in this: God knows you.

God isn't just a distant spiritual presence, off fighting cosmic battles or juggling planets on the other side of the universe. Jesus tells us, in the Bible, that God knows more about you than you even know about yourself. God even knows how many hairs are on your head. That doesn't mean that God has a big database of weird details about every human; it means that God knows your deepest joys and fears, your secrets that you don't even admit to yourself, your hopes and dreams. God knows *everything* about you.

That's not a reason to fear. That's a reason to rest, being aware that the God who knows you better than you know yourself is also completely head-over-heels in love with you. And even when you feel like no one in the entire world "gets" you or cares about who you really are, you can always sink comfortably into the truth that God knows you.

THOUGHT #4

YOU ARE LOVED

Think of the person or thing that you love more than anything else in the entire world. Now think about how much you love that person or thing, what that love feels like, and what it causes you to do. Now multiply all of that—the quantity of love, the feelings, the actions that flow from it—by a million. Or a billion. You're getting somewhere in the ballpark of how much God loves you.

Yes, God loves everyone. But that doesn't take anything away from how much God loves *you*. Just like a parent can uniquely and fully love multiple children, God knows you and uniquely loves you.

Still, it might seem a little weird to be so deeply loved by someone you've never even physically seen. There are things we love *in concept* more than in reality. You might "love" penguins, but you've only seen them once, in a zoo, on the other side of a thick plate of glass. So your "love" for penguins is more about loving *the idea* of penguins than it is a love for any particular penguin. (It would be a bit odd, wouldn't it, to have a deep love for one particular penguin?)

But God's love for you isn't broad and conceptual like that. God doesn't just love the idea of you. God loves *you*.

And get this: There is *nothing* you can do to make God love you less. And there is *nothing* you can do to make God love you more! God's love for you isn't in response to your goodness or badness. God's perfect love (remember: a billion times stronger than your most intense love!) is laser-focused on the you that he made and knows.

When you really understand this and believe this, it becomes a part of who you are (your "identity"). When you think about the big question "Who am I?", a central and true part of your response can be, "I am loved."

"AM I INFLUENCED OR FREE TO CHOOSE WHO I BECOME?"

Some people think they're trapped by their surroundings and parents and even the city or town they live in. They think they have zero choice in who they become, because all of these external people and places have locked them into a place of no choices.

They're wrong.

Others think just the opposite: They believe that no one has any influence on them. Not their parents, not their friends, not the part of the country they grow up in or their teachers or anyone or anything else in all of creation. They see themselves as 100 percent independent.

They're also wrong.

As you think about who you are and who you're becoming, be aware of this: There are absolutely people and situations that influence you. But those influences should never be seen as chains that remove your freedom of choice.

Think of it this way: You get a little puppy and work hard to train it. It's a certain breed known for its potential to be a great dog or a vicious dog, so you're careful to give it the attention it needs and the encouragement it thrives on, all while providing boundaries and protection. Your puppy grows up into a big dog. And as you ride your bike around your neighborhood, your dog loves to run with you. Sometimes people ooh and ahh and say things about what a beautiful doggie you have; other times, they look terrified, as if your dog is about to bite their faces off.

You have clearly had a big influence on your dog's behavior and personality (and so have its breed and other influences in your home and neighborhood). But could your dog still make the choice to do something horrible? Absolutely! It's a big, powerful dog.

Now, we hope you're not offended that we just compared you to a dog! Instead, focus on the fact that we've just said you're big and powerful. Your parents, your siblings, your community, your life experiences (good and bad) all have a role in shaping who you are. But you still have a choice in who you become.

THOUGHT #6

"GIFTS ARE GOOD, RIGHT?"

Maybe it's obvious to you that you have certain "gifts"— abilities and talents that are a natural part of who you are (even though you might need to practice them to get really good). Or maybe you don't feel like you have any gifts at all (but that's only because you haven't discovered yours yet). We've certainly met lots of junior highers in both of those places. We seen teenagers whose musical, athletic, artistic, or math abilities are *really* obvious by the time they're junior highers. And we've seen lots of other teenagers whose gifts don't become as obvious until they're a little older.

A big part of your teenage years is the discovery of your gifts.

But there's more to it than discovering your gifts! Think of your gifts as a tool—and tools can be used for good purposes *and* bad purposes. A hammer can be the perfect tool for putting a nail into a piece of wood—or a hammer can do serious damage when used in ways it wasn't intended.

Here are a couple of examples of what we mean:

Tessa has a great gift of humor. She's just super funny and can totally make people laugh. Her gift can be used to bring great joy—or it can be used to make fun of people and really hurt them.

Jake seems to be naturally gifted at computer programming, and has worked at developing his gift enough that he's written some of his own programs. Jake can use his gift in a way that helps people—or he can use his gift to write a computer virus that damages and destroys.

As you start to discover your gifts, think about the good you can do with them. And be aware of how, when used selfishly or without wisdom, they can be tools that bring suffering.

THOUGHT #7

"WHAT IF THERE'S STUFF ABOUT MYSELF THAT I DON'T LIKE?"

All of us are a combo platter of good and bad, strengths and weaknesses. As you travel the pathway of discovering who you are, you'll surely find some stuff about yourself that doesn't exactly excite you.

Maybe you struggle with a school subject that you really wish wasn't so tough. Or maybe it will become obvious to you that you don't have ability in the sport or instrument that you once dreamed of playing for a professional career. Or maybe you'll discover a part of your personality that bugs you and you wish you could magically change.

Start with this idea: Don't compare yourself to other people. When we compare one little area of our ability or personality to someone else, we usually miss the whole story of who we are *and* who that person is.

But beyond that, here's a good rule to live by: Focus on your strengths, and make sure your weaknesses don't create problems for you or others. If you focus on your weaknesses, it's unlikely that you'll experience much success. Discover your gifts, and build on them. Don't ignore your weaknesses; just give them enough attention that you keep them from inhibiting your gifts.

YOU ARE INDEPENDENT YET INTERCONNECTED

"I'm an individual, and responsible for myself!" Yup, that's true (or it will be, once you're not so dependent on your parents for stuff like food and a place to live and a ride to the mall). "And I don't need anyone for anything!" Uh, nope. That's independence gone too far.

"I need my friends and family!" Yup, that's true. "And I'm completely incapable of doing anything, or even *being* anything, without them!" Uh, nope. That's dependence gone too far.

Becoming independent is what the teenage years are all about, in a nutshell. You're no longer a kid, completely needing your parents for *everything*. Life might be tough if you had to go it alone right now, but you likely wouldn't die. Gaining some independence can be fun, and it's a part of growing up.

But this is one of those both/and things, rather than an either/or thing. We don't move from dependent to independent. Healthy and happy people are both independent *and* interconnected. In other words, they can stand on their own two feet and make decisions for themselves—they take responsibility for themselves (including the consequences of their choices). But they realize the importance of community, family, friends, and a church who support them (and who they can support).

THOUGHT #9

LIES ABOUT WHO YOU ARE

Culture has already told a ton of lies about who you are, throughout your childhood. But as you move into and through your teen years, these lies will massively increase. Here are some of the lies to watch out for:

You are what you buy. The truth: You are so much more than a consumer, so much wiser than those selling to you think you are.

You are what you wear. The truth: Clothes can be a fun way of expressing yourself, but they don't have to dictate who you are (or aren't).

You need a boyfriend or girlfriend to be someone. The truth: Most teenagers don't have a boyfriend or girlfriend, even if they they'd lead you to believe otherwise.

Whoever has the most toys wins. The truth: All the gadgets and laptops and gaming systems in the world won't actually make you happy. Plus, stuff breaks.

(If you're a girl) *Flirting and dressing sexy is the image you want to project.* The truth: Flirting and dressing sexy can create all kinds of problems, including convincing yourself that you're nothing more than a sexy flirt.

(If you're a guy) *Being tough and silent is the image you want to project.* The truth: If you teach yourself to hide your emotions, you rob yourself of important and good stuff in life.

THOUGHT #10

"WHAT IF I DON'T HAVE A CLUE WHO I AM OR WHAT I'M GOOD AT?"

If we divided the thousands of junior highers we've known into two categories, we could create two groups, pretty easily, along these lines:

- Group 1: junior highers who know who they are and what they're good at

- Group 2: junior highers who don't yet know who they are or what they're good at

And Group 2 would be *way* larger than Group 1. So don't sweat it—at all!—if you're thinking, "I'm supposed to know who I am? I don't even understand the question!" Be patient. The junior high years are the *first time in life* when most people start thinking about these questions. And if you're not thinking about them yet, no biggie.

But if you want to start wrestling with this stuff, you're at the *perfect age*. Try stuff. Seriously, try a ton of things. Don't worry about being great at any one thing. Don't sweat it if you don't make the "travel team." Just experiment, and see what interests you. You often won't know what you like (and even who you are) until you try new things. And—this is the cool part—you'll often discover things about who you are and what you're good at *in the midst* of trying new things.

A Story From Junior High Marko:

A few months ago I started attending a new school for seventh grade. I didn't know anyone. And to make it worse, my family is moving to a house (which is why I started at this school), but we haven't moved yet. So I don't even live near anyone from my school.

Trying to fit in has been really hard, and honestly, I feel lonely every single day. I've made a few attempts to make some friends, but it hasn't really worked out very well, and so far I feel like I'm just picking up a label of being a weirdo.

Today, though, was a new low. I'd seen this super-popular kid named Peter wearing clothes that everyone obviously thought were cool: just jeans, with a thin white crew neck sweater under a plaid flannel shirt. But I could tell that how many buttons were buttoned and how many weren't, along with the particular way he rolled up the sleeves, was all part of the presentation.

This morning, as I stood in front of my closet trying to figure out what to wear, I thought, "Hey, I have those same clothing items that everyone thinks are so cool on Peter. I could wear that." So I wore it exactly the same way, making sure I had the right number of buttons closed and the sleeves rolled up just right.

But it backfired. All day long, kids pointed at me and laughed. Really, I have no idea what I did wrong. At lunch, I went into a bathroom stall, took the sweater off, and just wore the flannel shirt in a boring, normal way.

At school, I can't figure out if I'm supposed to try to stand out or disappear. It's like there's a code that I don't have access to. Luckily, my church friends (and I'm not changing churches with my family moving) don't care what I wear. I'm glad there's someplace where I can just be myself without all this other pressure.

99 THOUGHTS FOR JUNIOR HIGHERS

WHAT'S HAPPENING TO ME?

EVERYTHING ABOUT YOU IS CHANGING

Don't worry, this isn't the kind of book parents give their kids to help them understand sex. So we're not going to go into a bunch of detail—detail that you would probably either really want or really not want! But the reality is that you're going through (or are about to go through) one of the biggest seasons of change in your body and mind and emotions that you'll ever experience, and we want to help you with some thoughts about it.

THOUGHT #11

"WHAT'S HAPPENING TO MY BODY?"

The junior high years are a *massive* time of change for the human body, and it's about a whole lot more than sexual development. Just compare a group of sixth-graders to a group of eighth-graders and you can see the difference, right?

You'll grow taller, the shape of your body will change (from a kid shape to an adult shape), your voice will change, your skin will change (zits!), and you'll suddenly grow hair in all sorts of places, not to mention all the sexual development stuff.

Maybe you're really excited about how your body is changing. Good for you! But most junior highers we've known are at least a little bit freaked out about it all. And understandably: You want to grow up (probably), but you hardly recognize yourself in the mirror sometimes.

Here's something important to remember as you look in that mirror: God knows you and loves you. And this change that your body is going through is a *good thing* (even if it doesn't feel like it). It's all a part of God's loving plan to make a way for you to experience the best life. Jesus promises us that he came to give us a full life— and to really experience a full life, we can't remain little kids. So your body is changing to get you ready. Your changing body is a clear sign of all the huge potential that lies inside of you, potential for an awesome and meaningful life.

Bottom line: All the change you're experiencing (or will soon experience) is normal. Even more than that, it's good. Really good.

THOUGHT #12

"I THINK SOMETHING MIGHT BE WRONG"

We think junior highers are about the most amazing people on the planet. We *love* junior highers. So we don't want you to read what we're about to tell you as if we're speaking down to you. We're not: We're shooting straight, because we respect you.

We've worked with thousands

(maybe tens of thousands) of junior highers. And we have never met one who, at some point, didn't think their bodies were developing wrong. Maybe you've had one of these thoughts:

- I'm too short.

- I'm too tall.

- I'm too skinny.

- I'm too big around.

- I'm getting too much attention because of how I look.

- I'm not getting enough attention because of how I look.

- All this body hair is freaking me out.

- I think I'm lopsided.

- My "man parts" or "woman parts" are too small or too big.

Junior high can be brutal because of these feelings. And it's even more brutal when other people point them out or tease you.

But here's the most honest and best truth we can give you (because it really is true in 99.9999 percent of the junior highers we've seen grow into young adults): You'll be OK. You might feel "abnormal" at the moment. But everyone else you know feels abnormal at some point, too. You'll turn out great, and whatever uniquenesses your body does end up with will matter a whole lot less very soon.

THOUGHT #13

"SOMETIMES I FEEL DEPRESSED FOR NO REASON"

We don't want to downplay the fact that plenty of people, junior highers included, have issues with depression that require medical help. And if you're struggling with serious depression (especially if you have attempted to hurt or have thought about hurting yourself in any way), please talk to an adult.

But almost all middle schoolers feel "bummed out" from time to time. "I just don't have any energy." "I really don't feel like doing anything at all. I just want to sit in a chair or lay in my bed." "I feel like I could cry."

And the really wild thing about this (you're not alone in this—it's common!) is that you probably don't have a reason for it, right? You feel mildly depressed or "down," but there's not much of a specific experience, conflict, or frustration you can point to as the cause.

We know it's *far from fun*, but there are a couple reasons for it. First, your body is going through so many changes, there's sometimes not much left over for perkiness. It's *physically and emotionally draining* to go through all the changes you're experiencing!

Also, your emotions are changing just like your body is changing. You had kid emotions, and you're growing into adult emotions. Kid emotions are like an appetizer compared to the giant entre of adult emotions. It's not that kid emotions aren't real; they're just super limited. But as your brain changes and you start to think in new ways, you also get to experience emotions in a whole new way.

Because all those emotions are a new experience, they can be overwhelming. So take a nap, or get some exercise. Get up and *do something*. Have a conversation with a friend. Or watch something that will make you laugh. Eat something healthy (lousy food can add to the feeling of depression, by the way).

THOUGHT #14

"SOMETIMES I'M SO HYPER, AND IT'S SORT OF FUN, AND SORT OF SCARY"

You've probably had an energy drink at some point and felt that surge of energy. Or even if you haven't had that, you can probably remember the sugar buzz you had that time you ate too much sugary candy.

But have you ever just felt *totally wired* for no reason? You get extra talkative (even to the point of annoying people), or just can't stop moving, or have an insuppressible giggle fit, or just feel like you're going to

WHAT'S HAPPENING TO ME?

burst out of yourself.

Ready for it? (You know what we're going to say here, right?) This is normal. Don't sweat it.

Just like the feelings of depression that can slide in from time to time for junior highers, feelings of energy or being hyper are just as common. You might experience more of one than the other (feeling "down" or feeling "wired"), but they're both coming from the same place for most teenagers.

It's those changing emotions, plus the fact that you have all sorts of crazy hormones racing through your body like a cat that's been guzzling energy drinks all day. (Can you picture that?) The feeling can be sort of fun at times. But it can also be a little disorienting.

Before you start labeling yourself a spaz or something, focus long enough to read this: You'll be fine. This is all part of growing into the emotions that your loving God is giving you so you can fully experience the best life possible.

THOUGHT #15

JUST ONE THOUGHT ABOUT SEX

Junior highers receive all sorts of mixed messages about sex. Probably more than at any other stage of life, you're sent all sorts of conflicting messages:

- "You're a teenager, so you must think about sex ALL THE TIME!"

- "All the cool kids are starting to fool around, and you're a loser if you've never 'gotten any action.' "

- "We fully expect that you'll start having sex very soon, but please wait a little longer."

- "If you really love someone, you're supposed to express that by having sex."

- "Sex is sinful!"

Here's the problem: All of those statements are either completely untrue or partially untrue. And all those mixed messages must sometimes leave you wondering if sex is a good thing or a dirty thing. It probably feels like you even get mixed messages from your own body!

Here's the totally true, no-spin, full story: Sex is great. It's one of God's coolest inventions. But what so many people don't realize is how *powerful* it is. And because it's so powerful, it can have wonderful results or horrible results. It can bring intimacy and connection to a married couple, and it can completely shatter lives when used carelessly.

So yes, your body is *getting ready* for sex. Cool. That's potentially going to be a really wonderful thing for you one day, once you're married.

THOUGHT #16

"PEOPLE JUDGE ME BY HOW I LOOK!"

One of the crueler realities in our culture is the number of assumptions made about people based on how they look. This usually unfair practice is probably stronger in our country than anywhere else. And it seems to ramp up big-time in junior high.

There's a reason for this, even though it's not fair and can be really hurtful. As your brain starts to become more like an adult brain (instead of a kid brain), you're beginning to see the world and everything around you in new ways. You're starting to see things (and people, and even yourself) from other perspectives. For example, the ability to imagine what someone else thinks when they look at you—that's a new thinking ability that you didn't have a few years ago.

But along with this new thinking ability, you and your friends start to learn how to make connections between categories. We mean no insult when we say this: You're not very good at it yet. Your brain is just learning how to do this stuff. So it's easy to make overly simple connections and generalizations that aren't necessarily true.

So the guy who's large and muscular is assumed to be good at sports, or even potentially violent (an assumption based on what we *think* those muscles could do). And the girl who has the body of a woman earlier than her friends is assumed to be sexually loose.

Of course, these assumptions are usually not correct, and when they are, it's often because the guy or girl is living into the expectations everyone seems to have about them (even if it's not who they would really choose to be).

If you're being judged based on how you look, stand firm in who you are and who you want to become. Don't cave in to others' (wrong) perceptions of you. And be extra careful not to put others in a box based on how they look.

"I'M STARTING TO QUESTION SOME OF THE STUFF I'VE ALWAYS BELIEVED"

It can be a bit trippy to have a great sense of confidence about what you believe (like: your faith), and then start to wonder if it's all true. It's a little like playing for years in a tree fort, and then suddenly noticing a few things about the tree that make you wonder if the whole thing might crash down at any moment.

Questioning what you've believed is normal, and it's a good thing. In fact, it's a super important part of you owning your own faith. And God isn't freaked out about this, or angry with you for asking questions or having doubts. In fact, God is the one who designed your brain in such a way that you would start asking questions and having doubts during your teenage years!

Of course, there are *good ways* to process doubts and *bad ways* (or not-so-helpful ways) to process doubts (more about this in the section called "How Do I Figure Out What I Believe?"). But *having* doubts and questions isn't the problem.

If you believe something that's not accurate, or not as completely true as possible, wouldn't you want to know? And the process of embracing a "truthier truth" usually includes some questioning about what you currently or previously believed. In that sense, doubts and questions are a helpful starting point, calling us to dig in and seek truth!

THOUGHT #18

"AND WHAT DO MY FRIENDSHIPS HAVE TO DO WITH ALL OF THESE CHANGES?"

Picture this: You take a medium-sized room with no windows, and you put a big tub of Legos® in the middle. Then you ask 10 little kids—let's say they're all 7 years old—to hang out in the room for an hour. Tell them you want them to build something with the Legos. They've never met each other before. And for a few moments, they hang around in the room nervously, wondering what they're supposed to do. But pretty soon, one of them digs into the tub of Legos—and before you know it, they're all getting along perfectly. Some work on their own, and some work together. But unless there's a little bully in the room who feels the need to destroy what others are constructing, it's a little haven of happy builders.

Now empty out the room and put the Legos back in the tub. Bring 10 eighth-graders (who've never met each other) into the room and ask them to hang out for an hour, building something. What happens? Will they all just get along perfectly, like the little kids? Or will the relationships and behaviors in the room have a whole lot more complexity?

Yeah. Complexity. Some will align themselves with a couple of people and start a conversation. Some will be super verbal, and others will hardly say a word. Some will dominate, and others will quietly follow along. There will be lots of posturing and posing, for sure.

The changes your brain is going through, as it becomes more of an adult brain, have implications for your friendships. You're aware of how others see you in a way that you weren't only a few years ago. And you're starting to get a sense of who you are (see Chapter 1), which means you're more likely to want to make friends with others who share your interests or outlook, and not just make friends with someone who lives near you or spends a

WHAT'S HAPPENING TO ME?

lot of time in the same place as you.

This shift in how junior highers make friends can be difficult to navigate. Just remember that it's all a part of a bigger change going on in your life, as you're learning, all over again, how to make friends and be in relationship with others.

THOUGHT #19

YOUR OWN PACE

Let's do another imaginary experiment. Take 1,000 junior highers from all over the country, randomly chosen. Now have them count off from 1 to 100, repeating the sequence 10 times. Then ask all those with the number 43 to step forward. You should have 10 junior highers.

Look at those 10 junior highers. What do they have in common? Could you look at those 10 and make a big list describing in detail what middle schoolers are like? Could you ask them a bunch of questions about what they know and what they believe and add to your list? Maybe. Maybe not.

The reality is that junior highers (you and your friends!) are *all over the place*. It's really hard to say, "This is a typical junior higher." Some are not all that different from kids. And some seem like they're not all that different from college students.

Every junior higher is going through massive changes

and experiencing those changes in unique ways and at unique speeds. You might feel like you're out in front or at the back of the pack. But from the perspective of your whole life (birth to death), it hardly matters—you'll likely find your place in a new normal after your teenage years are over.

THOUGHT #20

"I'M TIRED"

Yup, junior highers feel tired a lot. It makes sense, doesn't it, when you consider all the extra work your body and brain are doing to transform you into a young adult? God has wired you for a season of big change, and all of that takes energy.

Plus, now that you're getting older, you're probably staying up later. So you might be getting less sleep (especially during the school week). It's normal to feel tired during your junior high years. It's your body's way of saying, "Hey, notice me! I need rest!"

So sleep. A lot. It will refill your energy tanks so you can keep plugging forward on your adventure of transformation from kid to young adult.

A Story From Junior High Marko:

Last spring, as a second-semester seventh-grader, my

legs were still smooth and hairless. There were wispy, little hairs on them, I suppose—but you'd need a magnifying glass to see them. I didn't really care, even though I was certainly aware that most men have hairy legs, and that would probably happen to me at some point.

But then, about a month before the end of school, I noticed something: Dark, manly leg hairs were growing in. (I hadn't even noticed them!) But the weird thing was that they were, at that point, only growing in between my knees and my ankles, on the bottom half of my legs.

I think one reason I didn't notice them is because that part of my legs is normally covered up, even when I'm wearing shorts. In my world, all the guys wear tube socks that come up to just below their knees.

Here's the part I'm a little embarrassed to admit: I concluded that leg hairs must grow best in the dark, since the part of my legs that had them were normally covered up. And I wanted to have manlier, hairy legs— with hair on the top half, too! So as school got out for the summer, I made a decision: I would keep my legs in the dark all summer by wearing jeans—and never shorts.

It was a long, hot summer, and I was often uncomfortable. But I thought it worked! Because by the end of the summer, I had nice dark leg hairs all over, above and below my knees.

But I recently mentioned this to my dad, and he told me how I'd been wrong, that keeping my legs "in the dark" had nothing to do with it, and that my leg hairs would have grown in when they did no matter what I had done or worn. I could've been wearing shorts!

99 THOUGHTS FOR JUNIOR HIGHERS

YOU AND GOD

As you make the shift from being a kid to being a young adult, everything about your spiritual life—your beliefs, your relationship with God, and what it means to live as a follower of Jesus—starts to morph and shift. If you just let this happen to you, you might have a hard time holding on. But you can play an active role in pursuing a faith that's as mature as you're becoming.

THOUGHT #21

"WHAT'S FAITH?"

Let's start with this: You know what beliefs are. A belief is anything you've decided to be true. That doesn't necessarily mean it actually *is* true: You can hold to a belief that you have the superpower of invisibility, and just be wrong. But it's still a belief.

You come into your junior high years with thousands, maybe even millions, of beliefs. You believe certain things about gravity, pizza, clouds, Jupiter, and the fairness of the rules your parents have for you. And you have beliefs about God. Everyone does (really, everyone). Even an atheist (someone who believes that God doesn't exist) is expressing a belief about God.

Your beliefs about Jupiter probably don't impact your actions very often, but lots of your beliefs have a big-time impact on the choices you make. But the choices aren't the belief: They're just the result of the belief.

Faith, though, takes things a step further than belief. Faith is *belief in action*. You can believe, from the ground, that the high dive won't snap when you bounce on it, but it only becomes faith when you climb up to the high dive and spring off your toes.

So when we talk about a Christian faith, we're talking about the *way you live your life* and the choices you make, usually based on beliefs that are a little hard to actually prove (other than by exercising faith).

THOUGHT #22

"HOW DO I TALK TO GOD?"

What's the difference between someone sitting in a room and talking to herself, and someone sitting in a room and talking to God? If you observe both situations, you might not see any difference (unless the person talking to God is positioning her body or hands in a way that suggests prayer).

So talking to God—prayer—is an expression of faith. It's an action flowing out of a belief that God exists and listens. What does that mean for how you pray?

If you believe God wants you to try to impress him, then you might pray with fancy words. But God isn't impressed.

If you believe God doesn't really know what's going on

in your life (and mind), you might pray in a way that isn't honest, trying to trick God. But God knows everything about you.

If you believe God isn't insightful or powerful enough to help you, you might talk to God like he's a child, explaining to him what needs to be done. But God is completely powerful enough for anything you could ever need or face.

So talk to God with honesty, using your real voice (out loud, or in your mind—it doesn't matter). Talk to God with expectancy that he's listening. Talk to God with conviction that he cares about what's going on in your life.

THOUGHT #23

"HOW CAN I HEAR OR SEE GOD?"

Sometimes it would be nice if God would sit down next to you in a physical body so you could look him in the eyes. Or even if he would show up like a semi-transparent 3D hologram when you wanted to talk to him.

But no one could handle that, because God is so much greater than any image we could come up with. And we would quite literally die if we were exposed to *all* of God's goodness, power, and beauty.

But God really wants us to see and hear him. We just

have to know where to look and how to listen. We'll get into this in more detail in the "How Do I Figure Out What I Believe?" chapter. But for now, let's say this: Look for God in the places he tells us he's found. Look for God to reveal himself in the Bible. Look for God to reveal himself in nature (it's his creation, after all). Look for God to reveal himself through the lives of people who are living for him.

And listen for God to speak to you in all those same places, as well as through your own mind and heart. God's voice often comes to us as a thought, or as an image, or feeling like a suggestion from our conscience. When you train yourself to listen for God's voice, you'll get more and more practiced at hearing him.

THOUGHT #24

"HOW DO I KNOW THIS IS THE RIGHT RELIGION?"

This is a great question that we hear from lots of junior highers—a question that shows the progress you're making on owning your beliefs and faith. You're starting to discover that there are really intelligent people who care about spiritual things but have very different beliefs than you (or your parents, or your church).

There are all sorts of arguments for why Christianity is a set of beliefs that make good sense. But at the end of the day, those are beliefs, and other religions have good arguments (well, some of them do) for why their religion makes sense, too.

Two thoughts for you: First, focus more on finding out what's true than on convincing other people that they're wrong. It's not our job, as followers of Jesus, to decide "who's in and who's out." Our job is to follow Jesus.

And second, this comes back to faith (not just belief). Unless you step out in faith, putting action to your beliefs, you'll never discover what's really true. But when you do exercise faith, you'll find truth.

THOUGHT #25

"I DON'T UNDERSTAND WHO THE HOLY SPIRIT IS"

The concept of the Trinity is really hard to get our human minds around—that God is one God, but with three distinct expressions or persons. Even super smart adults who spend all their time thinking about this stuff find it challenging to explain!

Some people compare the Trinity to an egg, with three parts: yolk, white, and shell. One egg, three parts. Others have tried to explain the Trinity using the three forms of H2O: liquid, gas, and solid (ice). All water, three forms. But both of those examples still fall short of fully explaining something that is a bit of a mystery.

You probably have a good sense of God the Father and God the Son (Jesus). That leaves the Holy Spirit, the third person of the Trinity, and the one many churches seem to talk about the least.

The Holy Spirit (sometimes just called "the Spirit," and sometimes called "the Holy Ghost," which probably gives you the wrong image in your mind!) is God coming to us to comfort, to challenge, to encourage, to make us bold or give us strength, to guide us. When we talk about God "speaking" to us, we're really referring to the work of the Holy Spirit. When we say, "God gave me strength," we're talking about the Spirit's work in our lives. And same thing when we say, "I felt totally convicted that I was doing the wrong thing." Yup, that's the Holy Spirit, too.

THOUGHT #26

"I KNOW I SHOULD READ THE BIBLE, BUT IT SEEMS REALLY BORING"

We talk to so many junior highers who *want* to read the Bible, and *know* that it's an important part of growing in their faith, and even *believe* that the Bible has really amazing stuff in it that will help them in their real-world lives, but struggle to understand the Bible.

And if the Bible feels foreign ("This doesn't even seem like normal English!"), that's because it *is* foreign! The

Bible isn't really one book. It's 66 books, written by a bunch of different people (under the influence and guidance of the Holy Spirit), from a bunch of different countries and a bunch of different perspectives, over thousands of years! It's not like any other book, and the biggest uniqueness is why we sometimes call it the *living* Word of God: God is waiting for you, ready to reveal himself to you on the pages of the Bible.

A few suggestions: First, get your hands on a Bible that's in a translation you can understand (ask someone for help with this), and it's great to get a "packaging" of the Bible that's meant for teenagers, because it will have stuff in it that helps you understand what the Bible is saying.

Second, start with the stories. The Gospels (the four accounts of the life of Jesus: Matthew, Mark, Luke, and John) found at the beginning of the New Testament are a great place to start. Same with the book that follows them: Acts (or Acts of the Apostles). Those books have lots of great real-life events that aren't hard to read, and help you understand the life and teachings of Jesus and some of his earliest followers. The Old Testament books of Genesis and Exodus (the first two books of the Bible) also have lots of great stories.

Finally, ask for help. Ask a parent, a youth leader, or another adult in your church to help you understand the Bible.

"HOW COME BAD STUFF HAPPENS? WHERE'S GOD IN THAT?"

There is so much pain and suffering in the world. Now that you're a junior higher, your world is becoming much bigger—and with that, you're probably becoming more aware of other people's suffering.

That suffering can come in the form of a natural tragedy, such as an earthquake or a tsunami, killing hundreds or thousands of innocent people and damaging the lives of so many more. And maybe you've asked, or heard someone else ask, "Where was God? Why didn't God stop that from happening?"

Suffering can also come in the form of an evil done by people far away from us. "Where was God when that terrorist exploded a bomb in a plaza full of people? If God is really powerful, why didn't he keep that from happening?" And sometimes the most difficult suffering to face happens very close to home. "Why did God allow my mom to get cancer?" Or, "Where was God when that person did that horrible thing to me?"

These are difficult questions, and we don't want to treat you like a little kid and pretend they're simple. They're not simple.

The Bible seems to have a couple of important answers for us on this. One is that God often allows evil to occur because he has some greater plan than we can see.

Another reason the Bible offers is that our world is simply broken and in need of healing. This brokenness is our own doing (humans, that is), and God will bring healing and restoration to everything one day. Finally, the Bible makes it clear that God is *with us* when we suffer. In fact, our pain brings him pain, because he loves us so much.

Once again, we are called to have faith (not just beliefs) that God is good, and that our pain and suffering will, one day, all be a thing of the past.

THOUGHT #28

"HOW DO I DISAGREE WITH OTHER CHRISTIANS WITHOUT REJECTING CHRISTIANITY?"

A few thoughts back, we talked about the question so many junior highers have about whether Christianity is the "right" religion. But even *within* Christianity, there are so many different beliefs.

Choose almost any topic under the sun, and you'll find people who love Jesus but disagree with each other. It can be a Bible topic, such as "How are we supposed to baptize people?" or "What does communion really mean?" Or it can be a church-y topic like, "What's the right kind of music for a church service?" or "Should we have a youth ministry or not?" And disagreements are common around certain social issues.

We'll go into this in a whole lot more detail in the chapter called "How Do I Figure Out What I Believe?" But a few broad bits of advice here:

Ask questions and seek truth, but don't be a jerk. Remember that people who might disagree with you (or people you might disagree with) are *loved by God* and are made in his image. Learn to question without accusing or being mean. Learn to disagree while still showing love and compassion.

Then, don't reject what people believe just because you don't like something else about them. A snobby person can still be someone you can learn from. A person whose "style" offends you or bugs you can still speak truth. And we can all learn a *lot* from weirdos!

THOUGHT #29

YOU DON'T HAVE TO UNDERSTAND SOMETHING COMPLETELY TO BELIEVE IT

Do you completely know everything there is to know about the Amazon rainforest? Probably not. But do you believe that it exists? We hope so.

Do you totally understand how eyeballs and the brain functions of vision work? There's no way. But do you use your eyes, and basically trust that they provide you with accurate information? Of course!

How about snow: Do you know 100 percent of everything there is to know about how and why it's made and what each snowflake is made of? Be honest, you don't. But have you ever caught a snowflake on your tongue, or ridden a sled down a snow-covered hill? We hope so!

Even if you don't completely know everything there is to know about a subject, or completely understand every explanation, you can still believe it. We all do this *all the time*! So don't get all freaked out if you start to realize how little you understand your faith. Start with what you already believe, and move forward from there.

THOUGHT #30

"CAN'T I JUST BE A CHRISTIAN ON MY OWN, BY MYSELF?"

Sometime during the teenage years, and often during junior high, we see lots of students get bored or frustrated with church. They say things like:

- "I'm still totally a Christian! I just don't see why I need to go to church."

- "I'll probably enjoy church when I'm, like, 40 or something. But for now, it just doesn't seem like it's for me."

- "Youth group is cool and all, but I'm super busy, and

I think I need a break. My faith is a personal thing anyhow, so I'm good."

Does it work? Can you be a solo Jesus-follower—all by yourself and keeping it to yourself? Well, maybe, sorta—but not really. Following Jesus is a "team sport." Look through the Bible. Over and over again you'll read about *groups of people* pursuing God.

Your church needs you. If you don't hang out with other followers of Jesus, they are seriously missing out on everything you have to offer. And you need your church. Or make that: You need a church (maybe the one you're currently a part of, maybe another one). More often than not, it's other Jesus-followers who are the voice of God in our lives, encouraging and challenging, supporting and instructing.

We're not saying that going to church is a rule. It's not like that. It's just *almost impossible* to hold onto your faith without being part of a church.

A Story From Junior High Marko:

I've probably heard God speak to me before. But I don't remember any other times, before last week.

In my church, there's a youth group for high school kids, but not for the junior highers. We have programs that are OK and all, but it's not really a youth group. So the youth pastor is a guy I sort of know, but not really. It's more like he's my two older

sisters' youth pastor ('cause they're both in high school), and he'll be my youth pastor in another couple of years. Actually, if you'd asked me two weeks ago if he knew who I was, I'm not sure I could have answered, "Yes."

But last week I was cruising through this hallway in our church, and a bunch of people were in the hallway, because it was in between Sunday school and church service. The youth pastor (his name is Terry) stopped me. I actually thought I was in trouble and quickly tried to think of what I might have done wrong. But he put his hand on my shoulder and stopped me, and just said one sentence: "Oestreicher" (that's my last name—maybe he really didn't know my first name!), "you'd make a great youth pastor someday." Then Terry dropped his hand and walked away.

I just stood there, silent. I had this really weird feeling that it wasn't just Terry's voice I'd heard, but that somehow God was actually speaking to me. Funny thing is, I don't even like Terry that much, but I still think God spoke to me through him.

A week later I'm still thinking about it. It's much more than "should I be a youth pastor someday?" The much bigger deal to me is that I'm now way more certain that God actually wants to speak to me. And I'm listening like crazy for the next time.

YOU AND GOD

99 THOUGHTS
FOR JUNIOR
HIGHERS

THE LOW-DOWN
ON CHURCH

At times, the thought of church made us nervous, like the first day of school. It's not weird if you're still trying to figure out what church is all about. If it's new and you have a lot of questions, that's OK! And it's not weird if it feels comfy to you. If you started going to church before you could walk, you took your first steps there, and you practically have a name on the couch in the youth room, and you still have questions—also TOTALLY normal.

When you break it down, a Christian church is a place where we learn to be like Jesus. Church is an entryway for getting to know other people who love God or who are looking for God. It's a lot like glue: It holds us together.

THOUGHT #31

WHY CHURCH?

It might seem frustrating to spend some of your precious, non-homework time in a church building for a few hours each week. But God designed us to need community. God created us to love each other and to make much of his name. This type of community can meet all sorts of needs—not only our own, but also the needs of the people around us.

Being at church can pick you up when you feel like giving up. It can remind you of who you are and who defines you. It can help you decide what to believe and

THE LOW-DOWN ON CHURCH

how to act. The church is where you can discover how to study the Bible, where you can practice prayer, and it's a safe place to ask questions and get wisdom. It's a place where you'll find friends and leaders who will walk with you through stuff.

Big-deal life moments also happen at church. The people in the church (and that's really what the church is—not a physical building but people who follow Jesus) will bless new families when a couple gets married, speak words of blessing over babies when they're born, celebrate birthdays and big milestones, and help each other make big decisions or take giant leaps of faith. The church also cries together and remembers friends and family who pass from this life to the next life. It's a place where hurts are healed and unhealthy habits are broken.

THOUGHT #32

WHY DOES THE CHURCH NEED YOU?

When God created you and breathed life into your lungs, God gave you a unique piece of DNA that makes you different from every other human being on the planet. Even if you look similar to someone in your family or have an identical twin, you're still made for something only you can do.

You are the only you that God has ever made or will ever make in the history of the world forever and ever. Because God created you, your life has purpose—and that's a pretty big deal. God sings over you. God flat out has a party over YOU! (Check out Zephaniah 3:17.)

You may end up helping friends through a tough time. You may find that you have a talent that brings joy to others. You may sign up to be of use at your church. Or you may give your time volunteering or helping give energy to a movement that you believe in. Your trust will grow as you trust in God, and you'll be able to do so much more than you can even imagine (see what Ephesians 3:20 says).

CHURCH FRIENDS

We've heard teenagers talk about how hard it is to have faith in God around friends who don't have faith in God. But you don't have to be a different person with your friends at church than you are with your friends at school (or somewhere else). You can be you wherever *you* are.

Did you know that it's possible to share Jesus without talking about Jesus? Walk like he did. Accept others but don't become like them in their choices. Stay in touch with people who are more mature than you are spiritually, and have them keep you accountable in these friendships. God never asked us to hide out in the church. God wants us to share Jesus with people, and that means becoming friends with people who believe differently than we do.

THE LOW-DOWN ON CHURCH

THE WORDS OF GOD

Long before you were born, churches used music books instead of projecting words up on the screen or the wall. We would turn to a specific page number and sing together. But the song wasn't just the lyrics, like you'd find online. It was a musical composition with repeats and long notes and a whole lot of confusion.

You might feel like this when you hear God's Word read and talked about. Pastors and teachers who talk about God and God's Word do their best to make things easy to understand and remember. But even when we've listened to the best communicators in the world, we still can't remember EVERYTHING that we hear—and we may not understand everything the person was trying to express.

Next time you're hearing a sermon or a talk, listen and wait for a tug or an extra ounce of interest to grab your attention. Then think about that *one thing* (or maybe even two things) that you could apply, work through, wrestle with, or ask questions about. You don't have to track with everything that's going on. Just be open to learning, and you will.

WHAT'S A SPIRITUAL HIGH?

You'll probably experience times when you feel like you're closer to God than you've ever been. Maybe something special sparked that into motion, like a summer camp or a really great night at youth group. It's almost like you're on a mountaintop in your journey or have a lot of emotion and energy because of what's happened—a high, of sorts.

Having this type of emotion and energy is awesome and helpful, and it's a lot like a bridge that can get us to the next time of growth. Growth is like that: It often happens a little at a time, but also happens a lot at a time. It's different for every person. When we go through big "spiritual growth spurts" or have a big experience, we might go home or return to our routines excited and ready to tell others about what's been happening.

But we might not get the support we thought we would receive. Or we feel like no one understands. That's why it's really good to be connected to a Christian community—so the "spiritual highs" don't leave you wondering and doubting what happened. We need a lot of reminding, and being with other people who are growing to be more like Christ is super helpful.

THOUGHT #36

A REASON TO SING

In *The Little Mermaid*, Ariel has a bird friend named Scuttle. He's likable because he naively believes that he knows a lot about everything. He's a great friend, always offering Ariel the back story on different things. He names things whatever he feels like, and he makes up uses for a fork (it's a brush to him) and pipes (a musical instrument). He's super confident in what he thinks and in who he is, and no one ever seems to argue.

This same confidence leads him to serenade Ariel and Prince Eric with his awful, squawking singing voice. He belts it out—and isn't ashamed.

Maybe you're a lot like Scuttle—your singing voice isn't so refined, and it may even be painful for others to hear. But you can be like Scuttle in the way you confidently gather with others at church. You also can learn to be unashamed (if you aren't already) to gather at church and to grow as you sing (even if you "whisper sing"), pray, serve, hang out, eat together, and go on a journey together.

HEALTHY CHURCH

Church is full of people who are on the same journey that you're on. Some are older; some are younger. No one is perfect. But we can be healthy even with our imperfections.

Every person has a little bit of crazy in them. Every person has a story. We are still working on stuff and trying our best to get over our hurts and hang-ups—we are all works in progress. Sometimes this means that we could hurt the church with our words or our actions. When the earliest Christ-followers began to meet, some problems surfaced right away. Gossip. Drama. Selfishness.

But we can be kind to each other. We are meant to forgive. God wants us to see people's needs in our church and respond to them. It can be hard to do that when we are focused on getting what we want and not thinking about other people as an extension of Jesus' very own body.

So the way we can make sure we don't get sucked into living that way is to tend the fruit that grows as we have a relationship with God—the fruit of God's Spirit. Love. Peace. Faithfulness. Joy. Goodness. Patience. Kindness. Gentleness. Self-Control.

Let this stuff grow in you and you'll be the healthy church, together with everyone who looks for this kind of life.

THOUGHT #38

GOD SPEAKS

When you go to church, what kind of attitude do you take? Are you expecting it to be an amazing experience? Are you looking for God and thinking about God and wanting to hear from God?

You can have this same attitude at home when you read the Bible, when you talk with your parents, or when you pray. God's voice is thick and rich when Christians meet to connect with God and each other. Church amplifies God's call on our hearts by being a place of hearing God's Word, a place of meeting, and a place of sharing defining moments like birth, baptism, marriage, and even death.

When you feel like God is speaking to you, don't dismiss it. Write it down. Use the prayers found in the book of Psalms to sort it out. Talk to other people about it—and if God asks you to do something specific, try it and watch how God will continue to speak as you put some major trust in him.

SACRED DONUTS

If you've ever stacked up five donuts and ate them before 10 a.m. on a Sunday, then this nugget of wisdom is for you.

Food brings us together. Being together, we find strength. When we're strong, we're able to do things that require more trust. Trust helps us to take risks that lead to a rewarding faith.

That's why many churches use donuts to get that whole process started at 9 a.m. (when some early bird decided church would happen for junior highers). If the time ever changes to a decent wakeful hour, we'd buy hamburgers. But for now, donuts it is.

A Story From Junior High Brooklyn

Every time my grandpa goes to church, he takes us, too. I can feel the temperature of the wood chair-like pews where we sit, straight up. They're slippery, and I get bored. I try not to get sleepy but the person in front is talking—a lot. So I start daydreaming and writing and reading the information card thing, and then we play tic-tac-toe on it.

When it's time for communion, I wonder if I should drink that stuff. I'm praying every prayer I can think of: "Forgive me God," and "I'm sorry" for everything I've ever done in the history of ever and ever.

Is lightning going to strike if I eat this stuff without telling God every stupid thing I did this week? Is there an instruction book or something?

{Three months later}

I'm learning about Jesus in my youth group. I'm finding out that the church is full of a lot of people like me. No one is perfect. And there's a perfect person, Jesus, who we can get to know together.

I'm starting to understand what communion is all about now—and I don't feel like hiding under the organ anymore.

99 THOUGHTS FOR JUNIOR HIGHERS

HOW DO I FIGURE OUT WHAT I BELIEVE?

As you move from kid to young adult, one of the cool things your rewired brain allows you to do is make your faith your own. In other words, during these years you have an opportunity and a responsibility to figure out what you believe. Think of this chapter as a collection of mini-compasses to help you get pointed in the right direction.

THOUGHT #40

A FAITH OF YOUR OWN

It's not always true, but it's pretty common that children have beliefs about spiritual things that are a child's version of what their parents (or whatever adults they live with) believe. This isn't a bad thing—it can actually be really beautiful.

But if you become a 40-year-old with the exact same beliefs you had as an 8-year-old, you're going to find that they just don't work for you anymore. And people who do that usually end up with one of two results: Either they chuck their faith (because it *just doesn't make enough sense*), or they coast through life with a set of beliefs that don't actually impact the way they live. Either result isn't what God dreams of for you, and won't provide you with a foundation for the life of meaning and purpose that God designed you for.

So you have a big task ahead of you: figuring out what

HOW DO I FIGURE OUT WHAT I BELIEVE?

you believe! We hope (and we assume this is probably true because you're reading this book) that you're not starting from nothing. Even if you haven't yet started wrestling with what you believe, you probably came into this book with a basic set of Christian beliefs, and they worked just fine for you when you were younger. The good news: You don't need to flush them. They're a perfect place to start on this adventure.

THOUGHT #41

BELIEF INFORMER #1: THE BIBLE

There are lots of really good ways to seek out truth. But anyone who wants to discover God's truth needs to start with the Bible.

Maybe you've seen a TV show where there's a mystery prize. At some point, the curtain is pulled back and the prize is *revealed*. That's called a *revelation*. We see the same thing in movies all the time: We're wondering what's really going on, and at some point a revelation occurs, providing explanation to the whole story. Even people do this. With your closest friends, you've probably *revealed* more about yourself than you have with strangers.

God wants to *reveal* himself to you.

And the Bible is what people refer to as God's *primary revelation*. In other words, it's God's No. 1 way of showing you who he is, who you are, and how you can live to have the best life.

When you read the Bible, always ask yourself three questions:

- What does the Bible say?

- What does the Bible mean (in my world, today)?

- What is God saying to me through this passage?

THOUGHT #42

BELIEF INFORMER #2: THE CHURCH

Because God seems to trust us to develop our own beliefs (otherwise people wouldn't have so many differing beliefs!), Jesus' followers throughout history have had to *interpret* what they believe the Bible is teaching. Usually this is done through churches—groups of people who consider beliefs, dig for truth together, and come to some sense of conclusion about what's true and what's not true.

We can't ignore all the thought and prayer that has gone into the church's beliefs. This work has been done for centuries, and continues today. As an analogy, if you wanted to deeply understand airplanes, it would be foolish to never look at a plane, never read a book, and just start with a blank piece of paper and your brain. The same is true when it comes to developing your Christian beliefs. *The* church (all Christian churches, throughout history) and *your* church (a local group of people in a specific location) should be secondary only to the Bible itself in helping you know what to believe. That doesn't ensure that they're 100 percent right about everything, but it's likely they're *mostly* right!

THOUGHT #43

BELIEF INFORMER #3: EXPERIENCE

God isn't some mystical, out-there-somewhere idea. God is real and involved in every moment of your life. With that understanding, it makes sense that we can find God in our own stories, in our experiences of life.

Sometimes we see this best when we look backward. When you think about significant moments in your life, consider where God was in that moment—and what does that tell you about God and his character? Long ago (and in some places still today), Christian monks practiced something called the Prayer of Examen, a daily time to think back over the previous hours and consider the moments that brought them the greatest joy—and the moments that brought them the greatest discouragement. In each of these, they reflected on God's role and God's place in their lives. By practicing this form of prayer regularly, they found that they were able to notice God's presence more and more in the moment, and not only in hindsight.

Other times, we get a sense of God in the midst of doing things that bring us close to God. Maybe you've experienced this during times of worship, times of serving others, times of silence, or times of enjoyment with other Christ-followers.

Either way, our experience of God can be really helpful in forming our beliefs, because it helps us move our beliefs from our heads to our guts.

THOUGHT #44

BELIEF INFORMER #4: NATURE

Look at any invention, and it will reveal things about the inventor.

Farlo T. Farnsworth was a teenager who loved science and technology. He grew up on a potato farm and spent long days out on a tractor, actively engaged in farming while dreaming of science and technology. When Farlo was a teenager, people were trying to invent the TV—a piece of technology that could broadcast moving images through the air. No one was making good progress on the idea. But one day while on his tractor,

Farlo looked at the rows of potatoes and had an idea for broadcasting *lines* of color, rather than entire images. And that thought eventually led to the invention of television. Looking at an early TV would tell you things about how young Farlo thought and what was important to him.

If you believe God created the Earth (however you believe that God created it isn't the issue here), it should make sense that who God is and what God values would be revealed in his creation. That's why so many people often have a sense of God's presence when they're out in nature.

Spend some time in nature and consider questions like these:

- What does this tell me about how God values beauty?

- What does God think about life (and all things that are living)?

- Does God seem to be more into sameness and predictability, or originality and diversity?

- How do things in nature rely on each other, and what does that say both about God and about us humans?

BELIEF INFORMER #5: COMMON SENSE

You've probably had a parent or other adult say this to you: "Use your common sense!" Whatever their reason, they were trying to communicate: "You have a brain, and you theoretically have a general sense of what's right and wrong, so do the world the favor of employing all of that."

Good times, right?

Well, in the same way, your common sense can help you figure out what's true and what to believe about God, yourself, and the world. Common sense is merely the stuff that should be obvious to everyone. Anyone with what we could call a "normal" intelligence has common sense.

Who gave you your common sense? C'mon, guess. If you said, "Me!" uh, you're wrong. If you said, "I got my common sense as a prize in a cereal box!"—well, then, you actually do *not* have common sense. God (duh!) gave you common sense. God wired you with a basic understanding of what's right and wrong. So even the fact that you *have* common sense (whether you use it or not!) tells you something about God.

THOUGHT #46

BELIEF INFORMER #6: YOUR CONSCIENCE AND YOUR HEART

Have you ever seen a puppy that knows it did something wrong, and has a sad face that melts your heart? We connect with that response because we know what it feels like to have a guilty conscience. That sour feeling in your stomach, that pressure on your chest, that weight on your shoulders, that gnawing depression in your head—all of those are signs of your conscience kicking in.

That "guilty" conscience is only one of the ways our conscience works. You could say that your conscience is a built-in, God-given, internal moral compass, pointing in the right direction. If you feel guilty, it's because you went in a different direction than your internal moral compass was pointing—and it's letting you know!

The same is true of your heart. We're not talking about the big, blood-pumping muscle in your chest. We're talking about that center of feelings. Sometimes when asked why you know something to be true, your best answer is, "I just know it in my heart." That means you *feel it*, deeply.

Our consciences and our hearts aren't perfect. Plenty of people seem to be lacking a conscience (or have no problem overriding it), and the Bible makes it clear that lots of people have wicked hearts. But if Christ lives in you, your conscience and your heart become important tools for figuring out what's true and right.

WHEN DOUBT IS GOOD, AND WHEN DOUBT IS BAD

There's a famous passage about doubt in the Bible. Maybe you've heard it before.

After Jesus' resurrection, only a few of his disciples and other friends had seen him. But they had run back to where everyone else was hanging out being depressed and told them all, "Jesus is alive! We've seen him!" But one disciple, Thomas, didn't believe it. People have said a lot of negative things about Thomas over the centuries, but we think his response isn't that crazy. He basically says, "I don't know, guys. I'm having a hard time believing that. In fact, I don't think I'll believe it unless I see Jesus myself, unless I see the wounds from the cross."

Then Jesus shows up. Awkward! But here's the cool part: Jesus didn't say, "Thomas, you loser! You are *out* of the disciple club!" Instead, Jesus walked over to Thomas and helped him process his doubts.

We've said it already, but it's so important we're going to say it again: Your questions and doubts about faith are a *good* thing, even a *necessary* thing. They help you move from a little kid's faith to a faith of your own.

So, doubt is *good* when it causes you to seek truth, to find a better belief than the one you had. But doubt can be bad sometimes. Really, it's not the doubt itself that's *bad*, but our response. If we doubt and then just reject what we believed (the thing we were doubting) without seeking truth, we're allowing doubt to win. And that's never a *good* thing.

A Story From Junior High Marko:

Something happened to me recently that I'm a little bit embarrassed to tell you about, but what I learned from it is important. This past summer, I went on a wilderness trip with my youth group. We hiked through mountains, learned to do some basic mountain climbing and rappelling, and went whitewater canoeing. It was a great trip, but one 24-hour period was way harder for me than anything else on the trip. And the weird part is that I sat around and did absolutely nothing for those 24 hours.

After our two-week trip was three-fourths over, we found out that all of us were going to "do a solo" for 24 hours. That meant we were going to go off on our own—in the wilderness!—set up a little campsite (we didn't take tents, so the "campsite" was just a sleeping bag under a tarp, right out in the open!) and, well, survive.

I hadn't been all that afraid during any part of the trip up to that point, even when doing some really dangerous things. But out there on my own, I was terrified. So while I'm sure others hiked around their areas, explored, and did stuff, I literally laid down in my sleeping bag at about noon and stayed there for the entire 24 hours. And I didn't get to sleep until some insane time, like 3 in the morning or something. I kept twitching at every single sound in the night—and when you're in the middle of mountain

99 THOUGHTS FOR JUNIOR HIGHERS

67

wilderness, there are a lot of sounds in the night!

Somewhere just before 3 a.m., I started praying. "God, please help me calm down. Please help me not be afraid. Please help me know that you're here with me." I don't know how long I prayed, but I don't remember stopping, and I don't remember falling asleep. When I woke up, it was totally daytime, and I had a really cool sense that God had been with me all night.

That was four months ago now, and it has become part of my beliefs. I always had a basic sense that I could pray and that God would bring comfort. But now I know it.

HOW DO I FIGURE OUT WHAT I BELIEVE?

99 THOUGHTS
FOR JUNIOR
HIGHERS

FRIENDS

As you grow and change, friends take on an even more important role in your life. They become the people who get what you're going through and are probably going through it, too. Your friends have a huge impact on your everyday life. Being a good friend and making good friends is super important. So we've put together some of our best friendship help—stuff that we wish we would have known sooner, and stuff that we share with the students in our ministries. You're going to be an awesome friend. Read on!

THOUGHT #48

FRIENDS MAKE US STRONGER

I (Brooklyn) bought a house that came with its very own jungle. When we moved in, we started removing some of the overgrowth and quickly realized that it was going to take F-O-R-E-V-E-R. So we called a friend who coaches a college softball team. She rounded up her team and put them to work in our yard. In a few hours, they had removed tons (literally, tons) of jungle from our property.

The Bible talks about this strengthening effect. Imagine a cord or a flimsy string. You could probably break it with your bare hands. (You're burly like that.) Now imagine the same cord, three strands thick. It's harder to break. You may even have trouble cutting it with scissors.

God gave us companionship—one of the first things that

God decided to do. And the benefits are life-giving. Having a few good friends can make you stronger and can help protect all of you from the things that could break you.

THOUGHT #49

"I'VE CHANGED. NOW WHAT?"

You're coming home from youth group or a great small group time. Or it's the last day of camp. Or it's an event that really changed your mind and challenged your way of living. You're looking at your life, peering into the places and groups of people that didn't go with you to church or to camp or wherever you experienced growth.

You're thinking, "I've changed, but they haven't. Now what do I do?" It can feel a little weird talking about things with friends or family who didn't experience what we did. But we can't be afraid to let our friends know about an experience we've had and how it's changed our focus. It doesn't mean you're a different friend; it just means you might have a different destination, and that may need some extra communication.

Try to tell friends what you've learned in a way that doesn't exclude them or make them feel like outsiders. Try not to judge those who haven't walked on that same path yet. You'll have chances to share what you are going through, so be patient, explain, and surprise your friends with the same grace that you experienced.

THOUGHT #50

THE WRONG CROWD

"What do I do when a friend starts hanging with the wrong crowd?" Most of the time, this question is motivated by love and concern, but we're not sure what to do. Usually when someone refers to a crowd like this they are talking about people who behave differently than you do.

Did you know that Jesus hung out with the "wrong crowd" sometimes? But Jesus spent time with them in places where his integrity wasn't compromised (he was still able to live by his strong beliefs and also intersect with people outside of his beliefs and moral code). So it's possible to be around people who have a different way of life. Just be careful that you are wise about being with them at times and in places that won't cause compromise.

You may want to surround yourself with people who can help you steer through the question "Is it OK for me to be with this person or around this person right now?" And if you feel like a friend is beginning to drift into a place where the influences could lead to compromise, don't be afraid to put some distance there, while still loving them and caring for them as a person.

Ask genuine questions about how he or she is doing. Ask about the new things in their life. Spend time talking about what matters to them right now. Use your good listening skills to think of ways you can love that person or gently guide them to a place where they can make a better choice.

If something major is going on—a friend is in trouble or in a situation that may be more than they can handle—don't be afraid to ask a trusted adult for help. You may be the person that God could use to help that friend.

THOUGHT #51

WHAT'S A GOOD FRIEND LIKE?

We wish there were a "good friend magnet" that people could use on the first day of anything. Just think, on the first day of school, this magnet would lead you to the good friends in your class.

But because friend magnets aren't very realistic, let's think about the qualities of a good friend that you might be able to recognize in a person. Jesus talks about qualities that he would like to see in us as we grow in him—and these are also qualities that we would want to look for in others:

Patience: When you become friends with another person, you enter a period of time when you are getting to know each other and learning how to talk to each other, and this takes patience. You'll know when someone is patient when they stick with you even through tough stuff.

Kindness: You know you're on the good-friend path when the other person is kind to you and kind toward others. If there is a stream of negativity flowing out of your mouth about other people or out of theirs, you may want to find out why this is happening and work toward shifting into a more positive gear.

Humility: Good friends can have fun bragging to each other, or even kidding around sarcastically. But it can turn into boasting or talking excessively about themselves in selfish ways. When you see someone putting others first in a conversation or letting someone else have the spotlight, you're likely looking at a bona fide friend candidate.

Friendship is something that happens between people over time. Don't give up on being a great friend, and keep looking for great friends!

THOUGHT #52

BEFORE YOU QUIT

I (Brooklyn) was at summer camp with a few girls who'd been best friends all year long. Their group had been split up into different rooms for the week. A few new girls entered into their circle, and it changed the dynamics. Two days into camp, they started wanting "mini-conferences" with me about the new girls. They would come to me two at a time and talk to me about how "the other" girls were treating them.

We finally huddled up, and as we asked what was going on, it was clear that each of them was hurt. They all had legitimate reasons. Then we asked them if they could look at each other. They didn't need to understand or try to make things right or give any answers—just look at each other.

Somewhere early on in the week, there had been a feeling of abandonment from best friends. It wasn't intentional; it just happened. All they needed was a bit of extra help to get them talking and working through it.

You're going to have some moments when you don't "get" your friends. And you'll probably confuse friends with your choices and actions, too. But you don't have to let those moments end the friendship. Let them be an entryway for growing together.

THOUGHT #53

WHEN IS IT TIME TO MOVE ON?

We hope that you'll stick with your friends through the many situations that you go through together. Still, you may find yourself in situations where you'll have to make a decision about whether or not to continue a friendship. Ending a friendship isn't fun, but it can be risky to remain friends when there is evidence of danger.

A wise king who was inspired by God wrote this in the Old Testament: *The prudent see danger and take refuge, but the simple keep going and pay the penalty (Proverbs 22:3 NIV).*

It's important to think about the future as you build relationships. If you decide not to worry about the future and the friends that you keep, you may end up paying a price. That price could be a lot of things, but usually hanging out with a bad-news friend will cost more than you'll want to pay.

When do you break off a friendship?

- When the friendship doesn't add value (you're constantly hurting each other)

- When the friendship leads to doing things you'll regret

- When you're not yourself or feel the need to pretend you're someone else

- When you're uncomfortable or feel unsafe

How do you do it? Tell the friend who isn't healthy for you, "Hey, I don't think our friendship is helping us grow to be better people." Or you could say, "I'm not myself when I'm with you, and I need to find out who I am before we can be better friends." Or maybe say, "I end up doing stupid stuff when we hang out. We bring out the daring sides of each other, but I need to learn self-control better." It's always good to talk about how you need to grow instead of pointing out the wrong in the other person first. "I've been thinking about my actions and feel like I haven't been the best example. When we're together, I have the potential to do things I don't want to do. So for now, I think I need to chill out until I can better choices."

And you don't have to be rude to people who you've chosen to "unfriend" in real life. Kindness is free. You can offer it to everyone.

THOUGHT #54

GOOD-FRIEND GLUE

My 3-year-old (Brooklyn here) is learning to swim. One day she jumped in the pool by herself. We had to jump in and scoop her up because she didn't have a post-jump plan. Now when she wants to jump, she asks us, "Hey, will you catch me?" We get in the pool, she jumps, and we catch her. She puts all of her trust in us at that point.

When my husband, Coy, was a child around the same age our daughter is now, he didn't think it was necessary to ask. If he saw his dad in the pool, he would jump. One time when his dad was swimming in a lake, the toddler version of my husband saw the back of his dad's head and was certain that this would be a great time to jump. So he did. He landed on his dad's head but then slipped down into the dark water. His dad dived after him, scooping him up and saving him from what could have been some serious danger.

Coy trusted his dad that much! Even when his dad wasn't looking, Coy was 110 percent trusting in his dad. Trust is putting your confidence in something or someone. Trust is the glue to great friendships.

Jesus gives us this direction: *"Love each other as I have loved you" (John 15:12 NIV).* He says that we are his friends if we follow his directions and if we love each other.

Loving each other means putting our confidence in each other. It's laying down our own wants and needs in order to be able to help a friend out, to be there for them when a friend jumps, or even to swim around looking for that person when he or she needs extra help. Love is best displayed in the person of Jesus Christ. Watch him long enough and look for him deep enough, and you'll find that love is an action word and a movement.

THOUGHT #55

WHEN YOU NEED HELP

Maybe you have a big decision to make. The outcome could change everything. The choices are equally wonderful and terrifying (in a good way). You're trying to weigh out each decision in lists, in prayers, in time spent talking to friends.

Friendships are one of the biggest helps God gives us in life. Engaging friends in honest conversations can give you extra perspective. Sometimes we're too close to a situation to see that there are other options and other ways to look at things. Conversations also can help make you stronger. That's why it's pretty important to have a few friends who are looking for God with the same intensity that you are. Be a help, and offer help.

THOUGHT #56

STANDING FOR SOMETHING

You've probably heard the phrase, "Stand for something, or you'll fall for everything." Picking friends who stand together with you on some things helps keep you from falling for everything that comes your way.

That guy. That girl. That compromise. That decision. That temptation to lower your standards or weaken your expectations. When you make a decision to hold on to truth together with a few people, your decisions become clearer in relationship to that decision.

We all get hurt. Unfortunately, we take turns hurting each other. We get tempted, and sometimes we're the ones doing the tempting. It's not easy standing for something. But understanding something—that you're a new creation with directions from God to be changed—shifts how you act and react. It helps you make decisions when the world tells you you're not able to make them. Grab your friends and go forward in your understanding. Dig deep. Discover together.

FRIENDS DON'T FIGHT—OR DO THEY?

We really wish someone had told us at your age that friends fight sometimes. We're not talking about throwing physical punches (even though guys may wrestle more than they talk), but about the inevitable conflict that arises in friendships.

Because we regularly spend time with teenagers, we can spot conflict quickly. When sarcasm turns from playful to hurtful, we step aside and talk about it if we can. We say things like "Let's figure out what's going on here" or "Help me understand why you're feeling the way you feel." When people are ignoring each other, we encourage them to look at the other person and see them as someone they really care about—and then try to find out what's going on.

So if you're facing a rough patch with a friend, look for a chance to dig down deep and break the cycle of conflict. Show compassion—show that you suffer when someone else does. Let the other person know that your goal is to work things out and continue in friendship.

A Story From Junior High Brooklyn

My friend Megan lives in our basement. We have a big basement with a couch and a rug and some other things that make it look like a bedroom (sort of). On the other side of the basement are a washer and dryer, dozens of unmatched socks, clothes that need to be washed, clothes that need to be folded and put away, and our bird Jack. He hangs out in the cage that none of us wanted to clean so we put him in the basement to keep him from making a mess upstairs—and also to keep us from having to clean it out. He's been developing a weird growth on his neck. It may have something to do with the isolation and lack of clean water. Maybe we should be better pet owners.

Even with all of the weird things down there, Megan likes it. I'm not sure how it happened. We started hanging out a lot, and before I knew it, she was spending the night at our house all weekend. Then I'd ask if she could stay the night during the week. I'm pretty sure she lives with us more than she lives with her own family. We share clothes and go to my brother's baseball games together. And I introduced her to my cousins.

I live upstairs in a nice bedroom with carpet and clean air. I think she's getting tired of staying down there alone. Last night I went downstairs to sleep in a chair to keep her company.

Today she matched all of our socks from the laundry— and she gave Jack clean water.

FAMILY

Before your junior high years, you were kind of "along for the ride" when it came to your family. But as you move through your teenage years, you play a more active role in the relational feel of your home.

THOUGHT #58

"WHY DOES GOD WANT ME TO RESPECT MY PARENTS?"

Your parents' role goes way beyond their legal obligation to you. When God designed families, he had some very specific ideas in mind. But all of those ideas—just like everything God does—flow out of his incredible love for each member of your family. God's desire is that your parents would find great joy and meaning in parenting you (just as God finds great joy in being our Heavenly Father). And God wants you to experience the support, instruction, love, healthy boundaries, and (sometimes) correction that you need to grow into your full potential.

So, God gives specific roles to each person in a family. And your parents have a spiritual responsibility for you. In other words, God holds them accountable for raising you. You might think your parents are doing well with that responsibility, or you might feel like they're dropping the ball. Most parents are a mixture of good and bad parenting—because just like you, parents are imperfect people.

But God knows that parents not only have a responsibility for you, they also have more experience with the challenges of life. They usually have more wisdom and more knowledge. So when God asks you to respect your parents (which is an attitude that results in actions), it's because God knows it's best for you (even if it doesn't always feel that way).

THOUGHT #59

"MY PARENTS SEEM LIKE THEY'RE FROM ANOTHER CENTURY"

There's a good reason your parents sometimes seem like they're from another century: They are! Quite literally! Unless you're reading this book about 20 years after it was written, your parents were born in a different century than you. And even though your parents were once teenagers, they never experienced being a teenager in today's world.

Lots of things about being a teenager haven't changed from when your parents were your age: trying to figure out who you are, gaining independence from your parents, strong feelings, new ways of thinking, wondering about God. But lots of others things have changed or intensified since your parents' teenage years: social media, cell phones, access to information. And youth culture (really, the world you live in every day) has changed a ton.

So when your parents seem like they don't "get it," cut them some slack. Help them understand your world (you have to use words, and use them calmly). But don't be surprised that they'll often understand more than you think they will.

THOUGHT #60

"MY PARENTS FIGHT"

Living with tension, fighting, and conflict at home is really hard. It's not what God wants for you: God's desire is that you would experience a home with peace, joy, laughter, support, and encouragement. But even when the fighting isn't directed at you, but is between *other* people in your family (like, between your parents), it can create a home that doesn't feel safe.

A few quick bits: First, if you truly don't feel safe—if you are ever concerned for your safety—it's critical that you talk to another adult about it. Second, talk to your parents about how their fighting makes you feel. They might be defensive, or they might tell you it's none of your business (but of course, they're *making* it your business). But hearing your honest struggle might play a role in bringing change. Finally, when fighting breaks out, it's common for teenagers to feel very lonely. In those moments, imagine that Jesus is sitting there, right next to you, keeping you company and providing support.

THOUGHT #61

"HOW CAN I HAVE A GREAT RELATIONSHIP WITH MY PARENTS, BUT STILL HAVE SOME FREEDOM?"

Most junior highers we know really do want to have a good relationship with their parents. But they don't want to be one of those strange kids whose only friend is her mom. Most middle schoolers want an expanding sense of freedom, the ability to make more and more of their own choices, and some places in their lives where they experience privacy.

Those two desires—being connected to your parents but still having some freedom—don't have to be an either/or choice. You can have both. You *should* have both! And while it might not always feel like it, your parents want you to have both, too.

The challenge is that you probably have somewhat different ideas about what that looks like in real life. You probably (at times) want more freedom than your parents are comfortable giving you. And they probably (at times) want you to be more involved with the family than you want at that moment.

The key to this is conversation. You *have* to talk to your parents about the desire you have. Really, they'll just be stoked that you want to have a good relationship with them (make sure you express that part, too, not just the "I want freedom" part). And they'll likely understand your desire. So then it becomes a matter of ongoing conversation, talking about that combination, and listening to each other.

THOUGHT #62

SIBLINGS: GOOD, BAD, AND UGLY

Having siblings—older, younger, or both—can be awesome or a living nightmare. And as you move into and through your middle school years, your relationship with your siblings will change. Sometimes that change is good, like if you have older siblings who start to treat you more like a friend and less like an immature annoyance. And sometimes that change is difficult, like if your little brother or sister still wants a ton of your time, and you're not quite as interested in playing with trucks or dolls anymore.

Your siblings are a gift to you, and your relationship with them (easy or difficult, fun or annoying) will play a big role in shaping who you are, your strengths, and your ability to adapt to different people and situations.

Your newly rewired junior high brain has a *very* cool new feature: You can imagine things from other people's perspectives (you couldn't do that until very recently). This is a great skill to use in figuring out how to get along with your siblings—to see things from their point of view. If you exercise this ability, you'll get better and better at it, and it can be super helpful in thinking about why your brother or sister is acting that way toward you.

THOUGHT #63

KEEPING THE PEACE AT HOME

Your home *should* be the place where you can completely be yourself, where you can rest, where you don't feel any pressure to pose or pretend. But it's possible, as you move through your teenage years, that your home *won't* always feel like that.

We're here to tell *you:* You are massively powerful. You (yes, you!) have *so much power* to make your home a place of peace or a place of tension and isolation.

If you choose to spend time with your parents and siblings, asking them questions and listening to them, you're influencing the whole vibe of your home. And if you ignore them, are mean to them, or constantly expect people to serve your desires, you're influencing the whole vibe of the home in a completely different direction. Either way, you're not just changing the experience of home for yourself—you're influencing the experience of home for everyone in it.

This means that sometimes you'll have to choose a behavior or attitude that isn't your first impulse in order to get the much better prize: a home filled with peace.

WHEN FAMILY IS REALLY HARD, OR SCARY

Maybe you have a sibling who's making really bad choices that cause big-time problems. Or maybe you have a parent who drinks too much or has some other addiction. Or maybe you're yelled at, or told you don't matter. Even worse, maybe someone in your home physically or sexually abuses you.

If your home has any of these elements that make it seem scary to you, do two things: First, "make your requests known to God" (as the Bible says). It's not that God doesn't know about your situation: God is very aware of your situation, and his heart breaks for you. But there's something *very* powerful in asking God for help.

And second, please talk to a trusted adult outside your home. This could be a youth leader or another adult at church, or a teacher or school counselor. But if you feel afraid, you just can't keep it a secret. Even as we write this, we're praying for you, that God would give you courage.

THOUGHT #65

"MY PARENTS ARE AWESOME. HOW DO I BECOME LIKE THEM?"

There's no reason for this section of the book to be all doom and gloom! In fact, we know tons of junior highers who have a great relationship with their parents!

If there's something you like or admire about your parents, pay attention to that. Think about the "why" behind their actions—what makes them think or act in that way you appreciate? Ask them about it. And as you study both their motives and their behaviors, try them on for size. This can almost be like getting a really awesome hand-me-down shirt from your mom or dad, one that you think is totally cool. You try it on and see how it fits, how it looks on you. And if you feel like it works, you make it part of your wardrobe.

In the same way, you can try on the beliefs and behaviors that you like in your parents. Then, after a little bit of experimentation, you can make them your own.

A Story From Junior High Marko:

I bought my first album the other day (yeah, I know you guys "download" stuff in your day, but when and where I live, we still have to go to a store and buy vinyl). I had a couple of albums before this one, but they were gifts. This was the first one I bought with my own money.

I was so excited about it. My parents weren't home, so I put it on the stereo and cranked up the volume, listening to it over and over again for a few hours. I knew a couple of the songs from the radio, but there were so many songs I just totally loved. I loved how it made me feel: powerful and energized. The guitars ripped and the drums pounded, and the whole thing was all that much cooler because it was mine.

When my parents came home that evening, I told them about my album and how excited I was about it. And because I was so excited about it, I wanted to share it with them! So I asked my dad if I could play it for him. I knew it wouldn't be his style of music, but I still thought it was a chance to share something with him that I really loved—and he usually seemed to enjoy that sort of sharing.

As the first song was playing and I was grinning like a mad man, I noticed that my dad was not happy. In fact, he was actually looking angry, and musical style preference couldn't explain that. By the time the song ended, it was so uncomfortable that I stopped the music. My dad tensely asked, "Have you listened to the words? Do you know what the singer is talking about?"

To be honest, I really hadn't thought about it. I'd just been totally into the sound. But as we talked about it, I felt like an idiot: Of course the lyrics weren't great.

I've been thinking about this experience over the last few days, because it feels like two competing realities were being revealed to me: First, it was clear that my world and my dad's world are not the same. But at the same time, it was clear that my dad might have a point: The lyrics do matter, and he probably has some wisdom on that matter.

FAMILY

99 THOUGHTS
FOR JUNIOR
HIGHERS

FUTURE
MATTERS

If you asked us in junior high about the future, we'd probably tell you about our plans for the weekend. We may have had some dreams about our future, but they weren't detailed or mapped out with a strategy to achieve them (even though we know a few people who are doing this in middle school).

It's important to look into the future and think about how it's made up of a lot of decisions that you'll make right now. The future matters because you matter. We're here with you looking the future right between its eyes and believing that there's quite a bit we can do about changing it for good.

THOUGHT #66

THE FUTURE YOU

Everything in your life is changing more quickly than the weather forecast. Your brains, your body, your beliefs—everything is brewing up a beautiful storm of awesome adulthood.

"Ew, did they just say *adulthood*?" We know—it's not a cool word. We actually dislike using it to describe ourselves even though we've been adults for years now. Adults aren't like you. They're weird. But you secretly like a lot of them. The reason you like some is because you're going to be one.

Don't freak out, though. What we're trying to say is that

the future you is becoming and being built on who you are today. Every experience and chance to learn is building you to a place where you can become an awesome adult. Think about what you want to build your future on. Imagine what you'll be like, what you'll look like, who'll you be around.

The Bible says to trust God with your whole heart and to try not to lean into your own understanding—to accept God's authority in everything you do and he'll give you good directions (that's our paraphrase of Proverbs 3:5-6). The future you will be awesome. Just remember that the future is not so far away because it's being built with present moments. Take advantage of each chance to learn, grow, trust, and lean on God.

THOUGHT #67

"WHAT HAPPENS WHEN I MESS UP?"

We know of a middle school that has a "no cussing" zone. The signs make us smile because it reminds us how easy it is to forget who we are and what we should be about.

I (Brooklyn) wasn't a big "cusser," but my middle school best friend and I would get together and make up songs with only "cuss words." We thought it was fun—and it kind of was because we never talked like that and would be so grounded forever if anyone ever heard us talking like that. But it was a way for us to learn on our own what was good to say and what wasn't.

One time, I passed a note to a boy that was bugging me. It said something like "leave me alone," but I used words that were a bit more descriptive and colorful. The teacher saw my note and sent it home. My good self was wrecked by my own bad self.

My parents gave me some advice on how to handle the boy on the playground. (Just kidding!) They told me that I could express myself in other ways and wanted me to learn from the experience. I had to apologize.

Your future is important, so the moments when you mess up are important, too. Just accept your role in it, say you're sorry, learn from it, and leave it in the past.

THOUGHT #68

"HOW DO I EARN MY PARENTS' TRUST?"

"Why don't you trust me?"

We each used to ask our parents that question after they said we couldn't do something that we really wanted to do. But we experienced times at your age that taught us about trust—and that our parents were sometimes right!

Priority job description for parents: making sure their kids grow up to be responsible adults. It goes against their will and nature to let us do stupid stuff that might not guarantee our existence. One of the major characteristics of adulthood is responsibility—and if you are ready for more of that, then you need to prove it.

Begin by taking responsibility for things that maybe you haven't before. How about your household chores? Do you accept responsibility, do them, and not complain about it? What if you listened to your parents' instructions and followed them a few times in a row? It would begin to show them that you're ready for more.

The more you do this, the freer you will feel. Following your parents' lead will result in more freedom for you. Try it. It works. We promise.

THOUGHT #69

WISDOM FOR WHEN THINGS ARE OUT OF CONTROL

Waking up on the wrong side of the bed is the least of your worries. Your dad devoured your favorite cereal. You forgot you have a test in your first class. It's picture day and your hair just won't behave.

The friend you've played soccer with for years isn't talking to you anymore. You don't know what you did or said or what happened at all. Then there are the decisions that you make all day—little ones that pile up. And sometimes a big decision is in the mix. Life can feel kamikaze crazy like this, and when we feel this way, we are more likely to have weakened judgment.

Your body is telling you that you're tired, but you still stay up late anyway. The teacher lets you know about a project long before it's due, but you decide not to worry about it right away. Your parents aren't getting along, and there's nothing you can say or do to change what's happening.

Things can feel out of control because some of them *are* out of your control. Let's consider some specific things you can do when this happens.

Control the things that are in your control. Make a decision to pay attention to due dates and instructions. Do your best to keep these things in check so when other things get crazy, you won't be totally buried.

Pray for wisdom. James 1:5 says that if you need wisdom, ask for it, and our generous God will give it to you. Put your trust in God. Worry and doubt will cause you to waffle in your confidence. God has you, holds you, and wants the very best for you.

THOUGHT #70

HANDING OVER THE HYPER-SCHEDULE

The Internet makes it easy to take an extra class, be a part of new groups, and connect more. Connecting isn't a problem. But over-connecting could be.

You have priorities. You're becoming responsible. You're maturing. You're learning, and your brain is growing. You spend portions of your day with your family, with friends, or alone. It's tempting to be involved in everything. But not everything is beneficial for you.

Make a list of five things that you cannot ignore. Then write down everything else that competes for your time. Talk to your parents about how you can set some of these things to the side, take a break, or quit a few things to give your priorities room to breathe.

THOUGHT #71

WHO GOD DREAMS ABOUT

"I have a dream!" The man who famously spoke those words, Martin Luther King Jr., believed in the power of sharing his dream and calling others to pursue their dreams, too. He guided people to believe that his dreams of equality, decency, and respect could become realities. He saw something so vividly that others were able to see it, too.

When we're free and confident, we willingly admit that we dream about many things. We want to be great warriors and superstars. We dream of playing football in an arena or swimming in an Olympic pool. We dream of the day when we beat the video game and know all of the secrets, or the day when we finish all of the books in the series, or when we will get to take a weekend trip with our friends. We dream of family awesomeness. We dream of being happy.

Despite all your great dreams, God has an even greater dream for you. When God created human beings, he looked at the first one (Adam) and said, "Whoa, hold up now—it's not good for him to be alone." So God made a woman, Eve, to be Adam's helper. And God spoke some powerful words: "It is good."

God's dream from the very beginning was to bring out goodness. God dreams that you will be the good that you are—that you would know that you have been made with a purpose. God is looking for us to return to the good life—the place where we are content and confident that he continues to do a good work in you.

THOUGHT #72

KEEPING COMPROMISE AWAY

Limbo competitions are fun to watch. Every time the bar gets lowered, willing participants charge the bar—and at some point, everyone but the winner will fall, face plant, and fail in other entertaining ways. With the exception of a few very flexible people, the limbo breaks us all. And even those with abilities that resemble an elastic rubber band struggle when the bar gets too low.

Compromise is sort of like that. It happens in those moments when we lower our standards or when something weakens our beliefs.

I (Brooklyn) decided to give up desserts once in an attempt to eat a healthier diet. But I began to lower the bar by saying things like, "Chocolate is from cocoa, which is from a bean, so in essence chocolate is a legume" and I'd justify eating it—knowing that this lowering of my standard opened the door and weakened my desire to eat healthier. It shouldn't have shocked me that I started eating pancakes for breakfast with whipped cream and sprinkles and syrup (all sugar) and believing that it really wasn't dessert because it was "breakfast." I was my own worst enemy by lowering the standard, meal by meal.

How about you? What morals have you chosen to live by? And what decisions have you made that could place you in a position of weakness if you continue to lower the bar? You can always start again, right now! Defeat doesn't have to define you. Raise the bar one more time.

PRESSURE-COOKER CHOICES

Embarrassment is the gut grenade of the middle school years. Being embarrassed is *no bueno*. We may do crazy stuff on purpose and invite some laughter—we ask for it and expect it. But when embarrassment comes unexpectedly, boomeranging into our world without an invitation, it can leave a mark.

Sometimes we lower our standards because of embarrassment. We're afraid that if we do the right thing or change the pattern, we won't be liked, loved, accepted, included, or have a purpose. The Bible tells us that God doesn't give us a spirit of being hesitant or fearful. Instead, God gives us a spirit of power, love, and self-control.

You can choose paths based on the caution signs, on the things you're learning as you pray. You can stand up when you're under pressure to lower your standards or compromise. You can stand out as someone who is confident in *who* you are and in *whose* you are.

THOUGHT #74

BEING YOURSELF

It took each of us way too long to discover that to be accepted, included, and loved, we could make choices on our own and that those choices didn't have to be the same choices that everyone else makes. (But now that we know this, Marko is totally comfortable wearing a cat with laser eyes on his shirt and Brooklyn isn't afraid to pretend she is French.)

Choices go way beyond "what to wear," but the idea is

the same. If you have given God the go-ahead to lead your life, you'll make choices that set you apart (that's what the word *holy* means). When you read the Bible, you discover truths and ideas that you can build your choices on—words and insights from people who have come before us, God-followers who knew the secret.

God is there, ready to help; I'm fearless no matter what. Who or what can get to me? (Hebrews 13:6 THE MESSAGE).

A Story From Junior High Brooklyn

I begged my mom to buy the shorts with the hole in them. They were defective—not the kind of jean shorts that are meant to have holes, but the kind where they ripped as someone was trying them on. But it was my only hope. They were too pricey for our family's budget. I was thinking, "Maybe we could get a discount because there was a hole in them." My mom asked, "You want me to buy a pair of shorts with a hole in them?" Yes. I did. I wanted them BAAAAADDD. I wanted to have a pair of Guess® shorts (even if they were pink and hole-y).

We ended up getting the discount. I took the shorts home. I wore them for years thinking that having them made me more special. What I didn't know that I already was special. And the shorts really had nothing to do with that at all.

WHAT'S MOST IMPORTANT?

FIGURING OUT PRIORITIES

Think of the food pyramid you probably learned about in school at some point: Veggies are more important than, say, butter or sugar. In other words, vegetables are the priority.

You also have priorities—certain things that are more important to you than other things (even if the less important things are still important). This chapter is about how to think through that list: What should be the most important of the most important stuff?

THOUGHT #75

"WHO AM I?"

That's an important question to consider. You're looking around and the world doesn't seem as black-and-white as when you were a kid. You'll hunt for the answer to this question in a lot of ways. You'll look to your family, to your friends, and you'll search for things that fit—trying on and taking off, adjusting and adapting.

When we look at the awesome middle schoolers in our lives and see them searching for meaning and wanting to know where they fit, we encourage them to look in a mirror and recognize that God put really good stuff in there. Because it's the truth that they should know. And you need to know it, too.

You are God's creative work. You don't have to conform to what anyone else is doing. You only need to listen to

God's voice and answer it. That voice reveals who you are. It's the truth of God's Word. It's the nudge of God's presence in you. Lean into it and look for it in healthy adult role models.

THOUGHT #76

"WHOSE AM I?"

You might be referred to by your last name. People may know you because of the street you live on, the team or club you belong to, or the car you drive. And you belong to someone greater than any family ties, greater than all of the world's possessions.

Consider what the Bible tells us in John 1:12 (NIV)—*Yet to all who did receive him, to those who believed in his name, he gave the right to become children of God.* You have an immense family with a Father in heaven who gives you personality traits that reflect his character. You have access to God's incredible riches as his son or daughter. Knowing this can really shape you and change how you feel about your circumstances.

THOUGHT #77

A PERSON OF CHARACTER

Have you ever played with a puppy that was just naughty by nature? Let's rephrase that question: Have you ever played with a puppy that *wasn't* naughty by nature?

Puppies are a hot mess.

As they get bigger and older, they learn how to control themselves. They stop eating things they shouldn't eat and they begin to calm down (a little). It's in a dog's nature to be mischievous, playful, protective, and social.

We also have a nature. God created us with a pure nature of goodness. Regrettably, this goodness was wrecked by a sinful nature that draws us to choose wrong. So here we are, all of us, falling short in good nature, falling short of God's glory.

But God offers us a gift: the chance for a restored nature and a new life through his Son, Jesus. The good life starts the day you accept God's gift, and that good life never ends. God begins by shaping our character, our nature—transforming, renewing, and restoring our hearts and minds back to goodness.

Your character doesn't have to be owned or limited by anyone else's judgment. God has the power to work in your life to develop your character—the mental and moral qualities that make you more like Jesus, the image of God walking with us.

STREET CREDIBILITY

This book would have zero street credibility if we didn't have integrity. Why would you believe anything we're saying if we had a record of wrongdoing or a liking for lying? Being a person of integrity means having a habit of honesty, a desire for decency, a searching for sincerity. And when we make mistakes, we do our best to make it right. We aren't perfect, but we're doing our best to live up to the same standards we are asking you to think about.

If you're interested in getting an integrity injection of your own, you can—by asking God to help you. Pray about it. Talk about it. Read about it. Look for it in other people.

We learned from watching and observing adults around us when we were in junior high. When we could see that they were honest, trustworthy, decent, or caring, we would start taking mental notes.

Keep watch over your life. Look for leaders to learn from. Leave the old life in the dust.

Keep vigilant watch over your heart; that's where life starts. Don't talk out of both sides of your mouth; avoid careless banter, white lies, and gossip. Keep your eyes straight ahead; ignore all sideshow distractions. Watch your step, and the road will stretch out smooth before you. Look neither right nor left; leave evil in the dust (Proverbs 4:23-27 THE MESSAGE).

THOUGHT #79

SHOCK YOUR FAMILY

Want to make your parents pass out? Put them first.

That's right. Do what they least expect, and floor them with goodness. It's hard, especially if you don't get along all of the time. But the people in your family are the closest people to you—your parents (or stepparents) and your siblings (if you have them).

God calls us to love him with everything in us and to love our neighbors just as we love ourselves. But that doesn't just mean the people who live next door. Your family members are your "neighbors," too.

Make a love list. Put your family members first. Practice loving them through your actions. Be generous with each of them. Spend time together. As you do this, God will strengthen them and strengthen you. God is pleased when you put the needs of others ahead of your own needs. Give God the chance to show off in the ways you love your family today.

WHAT'S MOST IMPORTANT?

THOUGHT #80

LOVE GOD

Love can be a noun or a verb. When it's a verb, it implies action. It's easy to say that we love God, but what in our lives reveals that this is true?

Loving God is not like loving other things. You may love your new headphones or shoes. But nothing compares to loving someone so much that it changes who you are and how you live.

It's more than an obsession or a fad that comes and goes. It's a desire to honor and give your life to God in ways that express thanks.

This is God's plan for you, that you would love him. Like any relationship, your relationship with God will grow as you respond to the love he has shown.

THOUGHT #81

LOVE OTHERS

Audrey Hepburn, a famous actress from the 1950s and 1960s, is credited with saying something wise and tasty: "Let's face it, a nice creamy chocolate cake does a lot for a lot of people; it does for me."

You may enjoy gift giving (we're pretty certain you enjoy gift receiving!), but loving others goes a little deeper than chocolate cake and gift exchanges. What does it mean to love other people? How do you love someone you don't even know anything about?

Become a master of the moment. Look around and see how you can be generous to the people who are closest to you. Pay attention to details—and if the moment requires cake, then bake or buy a cake!

THOUGHT #82

BE A SUPERFRIEND

Here are some secrets to being a "superfriend."

Have a tenacious willingness to be a friend, look out for your friends, forgive your friends, be there for them when they need you, let kindness rule, and don't give up when you clash or have disagreements.

The best friends in our lives haven't let us give up on those friendships. And we do the same for them—even though it requires a lot of patience and selflessness. It takes time to learn these things, so stick with your best friends as they are learning, too, knowing that you're preparing for a lifelong journey.

Friends come and go, but a true friend sticks by you like family (Proverbs 18:24 THE MESSAGE).

MISS OR MR. GENEROSITY

A few years ago, a girl in Brooklyn's youth group learned the secret of generosity. She was 12 years old when she heard about people who didn't have access to clean water. She wanted to give money to help, but she didn't have any to give.

So she decided to use her sewing skills to make a handmade hanging bird. Since then, she's earned over $50,000 selling these birds and has helped provide water for thousands of people.

Her biggest sacrifice over the years has been time, as she's quietly worked for others. And it has sparked a determination in everyone who lives close to her to live generously, too. Generosity started in her heart with the desire to share with other people, even people she may never see or meet.

The Bible says that each one of us ought to give generously and cheerfully. God loves it when we give with that kind of attitude.

A Story From Junior High Brooklyn

My volleyball coach is giving us a talk. He's saying we should focus on four priorities: God, family, schoolwork, and volleyball. They should rank in that order. Nothing else should take the place of those things.

He has me thinking. How do I make God a priority? I'm not even sure what my coach means by that. Volleyball is the easy one, of course; it's a priority because I love it! But the rest, meh, I guess they're important.

Because he's my coach, I'll try it. I heard there was a good youth group going on now at my grandpa's church. Maybe I can get a ride there this week.

99 THOUGHTS
FOR JUNIOR
HIGHERS

YOUR CRAZY
LIFE

You have a lot going on. Even if you're keeping it simple—school, homework, eat, sleep—that's still a lot to fit into one day. Add church or club activities, practices, rehearsals, and lessons—you get another layer. Heap on a friend layer. Sprinkle on a side of responsibility (washing your family car, cleaning the bathrooms at home, loading and unloading the dishwasher, babysitting your siblings) and suddenly you have a full-on crazy concoction.

Take this life and dish it up with the cherry on top—a helping of social media. Now you've got a lot of fun (or a lot of stress) on your hands. Let's talk about how to manage the crazy life, one step at a time.

THOUGHT #84

TACKLING CHAOS

Everyone gets an agenda on the first day of middle school. So fresh and so clean. Ready for you to write your assignments and your responsibilities. Maybe you enjoy writing things down and check them off. Or maybe you've never even tried controlling the chaos.

Being organized helps. It keeps things in a state of control instead of a state of confusion and chaos. Maybe you have friends who don't write things down, but they'll draw pictures or leave sticky notes as reminders. That's what works for them.

Everyone can find his or her own way to be organized. The key is finding and following a way. Each act of organization is another step away from chaos. What's your favorite way to stay organized?

RESPECT BOUNDARIES

Ski trips are fun—particularly ones that don't end with anyone suffering from a broken collarbone. It seems like way too many churches take their trips when there's way too much ice, resulting in broken wrists, broken hands, broken collarbones, twisted ankles, and even fractured skulls. (Ouch!) These kinds of trips remind us that it's important not to go out of bounds and that respecting boundaries could mean keeping a limb.

If life were a ski slope, you would still see boundaries around you—areas that are more difficult, areas filled with rough spots, and clearly marked "out of bounds" places. We're wise if we look for safety when we see danger. And we're naive if we see danger but decide to keep going.

Think about your boundaries—the ones you've made and the ones established by people who love you (including God). Pay attention to places of caution, and make sure to find safety or make changes when you realize you're out of bounds in some area of your life.

THOUGHT #86

SELF-EXPRESSIONS

Smile! Go ahead and pose for selfie #568 of the year. You love expressing yourself. Whether it's your outfit for school, your weekend plans, your new puppy, or some other awesome moment, you like sharing who you are with others.

It's interesting that most of the time these photos and these experiences are recorded in bedrooms, bathrooms, backyards, and other behind-the-scenes places. Why does it feel so weird to be that silly self in front of your parents? It's who you are sometimes, but not all the time.

You can begin to introduce your social-media self to your real-life self. Is this the person you want to be? Think about whose attention you are seeking, and if you really desire that attention, think about how you can talk to that person or that group in real life. When you're at home, give your social self a chance to speak up—and when you're being social online, show people the diversity of who you are.

MANY SIDES OF YOU

Hyperactivity comes out in Brooklyn when she's in big groups with loud music. (Yes, we're intentionally talking about her in the third person.) It's the perfect situation for likes-to-dance Brooklyn. But she rarely comes out around shy people, including her husband. She doesn't want to make them feel uncomfortable with that out-there-ness, so she adjusts into a more mild person.

Which Brooklyn shows up in other situations? Well, at the beach, Brooklyn could spend eight hours alone. Quiet. Reading. Listening. Thinking. Drawing. When she's with her brother, they do adventurous stuff together—and laugh about all of the times they almost got in big trouble together. And if she's with her sisters, their personalities shift when they get together.

Her family brings out the "fun haver" side. She's a Disney® fan and a parade watcher. She cries during fireworks and wishes she were a kid again. Seeing little kids think they are pirates and princesses causes serious mental shifts for everyone (or so she thinks).

So are all of these sides real and authentic? Yes! You probably have many of your own, too. You'll learn that it's safer to share some sides of you in certain places—and protect them at other times. It's not being a hypocrite or two-faced—it's being wise!

When your knowledge of who you are is found in your relationship with Jesus, who never changes or wavers, you're able to be in rock solid to your core. You're a special person—unique and knit together with purpose by the one and only God who created everything you've ever seen or felt that is good. The real you is brought to life when you really love God. You are God's child, protected and purposed, and this person goes everywhere your "many sides of me" go.

THOUGHT #88

KILL SOME DRAGONS

You may not realize it, but you've met a few dragons already. They're the things in your life that seem to sneak up and devour you: homework, school projects, practicing for that big deal, the chore that you despise, the responsibility that you wish would just jump off a cliff and disappear forever.

They're your dragons because you don't want to go near them. But you have to—and you can take care of them, killing them and stomping them out.

The best advice we've ever heard about dragons is to slay them early. Instead of waiting until the last minute to do the things you like doing least, do them first. Then you'll have the rest of the day to do things that you *really enjoy.* The dragons are gone, the dread is gone, and the stress all day over that one thing that's breathing down your neck—it's GONE!

POWERFUL WORDS

The wisdom of the great King Solomon reveals that words have the power of life and death (go check out Proverbs 18:21). Our choice of words can determine what lives and dies? That's epic!

How you use words changes things. The best gift you can give to others is a positive word that says, "I love ya even if I don't know ya—and especially if I know you well, with all your faults!"

When our words are foul or offensive or rude, we hurt people who (just like us) are created in God's image. Try this: word swap. When you hear yourself using words that don't help bring life to others, put them in mental jail with a life sentence. Tell someone so you're not tempted to bail those words out for use again.

Exchange the imprisoned words for freedom words that bring people to life. Make a list of these words, and make sure to practice them with the people closest to you.

THOUGHT #90

CAUTION (WHAT WE SAY OR POST COULD LIVE FOR A LONG TIME)

Did you know that anything you post online can live on forever with a simple screen capture? Words don't just have power. They have legs, too. They move and carry things further than we could ever imagine.

Being careful about what you post publically online is important, not just for today, but also for your future. Future relationships. Future jobs. The things we say and the images we share reveal more about us than we might realize—so guard your media.

If you are unsure about posting something or about its appropriateness, then you're probably on the right track and might want to not post it.

THOUGHT #91

A LITTLE RESPECT FOR SOCIAL MEDIA BOUNDARIES

Making your social media profiles private is a good step. But there are still ways for people to see your patterns: where you live, go to school, where you hang out. Don't feel like you have to share everything that's happening in your life. Live your life *in* your life!

Parents may have given you some rules about your online interactions and activities. Some parents decide to not let their kids have a phone until they are older. Some people your age get devices but have security or restrictions. Others have more freedom with few restrictions.

Because the world is filled with all sorts of parenting types, know what your parents want from you and respect it—even when you have access to something through your best-friend's phone or computer. Remember those boundaries we talked about earlier? They're meant to keep you safe. Your integrity grows and you can prove that you're becoming responsible when you pay attention to the guidelines your parents have set up for you.

YOU ARE WHAT YOU POST

Brooklyn's Instagram® account is populated with pics of her kids, desserts, and bacon. She loves all of these things. If you didn't know her but looked at her account, you could make an educated guess that she likes her children—and that good food, especially bacon, holds a special place in her heart.

If you looked at Marko's pics, you'd conclude that he is wise indeed—his epic beard is proof.

What you post online is like a giant billboard telling the world about who you are and what you care about. Taking pics of our bods? May sound like a good idea today. It may bring temporary attention with likes and comments. But if you're looking for friendships and relationships that will honor you and your body, then those kinds of pics may not help you.

Decide what you want to say—and consider how it's communicated through what you post.

A Story From Junior High Brooklyn

I really like talking to my best friend on the phone. I get tired talking on the phone at night, but I don't want him to think that I don't like him, so we keep talking until there's nothing to talk about anymore. I'm not sure how to end the convo, you know? I don't know, so I just hang out there in silence, listening to music sometimes to keep him from hearing me slip in and out of sleep. What if I start snoring? I should be sleeping. Mom is going to kill me.

This morning, it takes three attempts for her to wake me. I'm so tired that I feel like I could sleep for the whole day. But I have to go to school and think about science. I don't like admitting it, but she was right: I needed to go to bed when she told me to. Now I'm tired, and grumpy, my socks don't match and I forgot my violin and my kneepads for volleyball practice. To add fuel to this tired fire, my best friend tells me that I snore when I sleep. Wow. Nightmares really do come true.

GIRLS AND
GUYS

When you were babies, we huddled you up in play groups. We didn't mind it when you snuck a toddler kiss or held hands or traded toys. You played in the sprinkler wearing absolutely nothing. We laughed and took pictures and bundled you up in towels.

When school started, we decided it was time to make sure you knew that boys and girls are different. But we may not have given you a lot of reasons why, because you were too young to understand some of it. But now you're older. We think that you can handle it. We think you can respect the opposite gender. We're certain that you have what it takes to honor each person's life and dignity.

THOUGHT #93

OFFER GRACE AND RESPECT

Guys and girls are different. But both are made of the same stuff and are created with the same purpose in mind.

Thinking about the things you have in common will help you as you learn to understand the opposite sex. It might just be super weird and confusing on some days, and you'll need to hold on to what's *always* true until you can understand the things that may *not* always be true.

Knowing that both of you are in process helps to take it easy on each other. Believing that you are both made of the same dust and created with the same good things in mind can help you when you don't get why she's acting strange or why he's not as talkative as he used to be.

Girls, give guys big piles of grace as they are growing. Guys, give girls the same and you'll build a mutual respect that can lead to healthy friendships and better understanding in the future.

THAT BUBBLE SPACE

In kindergarten, students are taught to stay in their own bubble space. At a young age, we're taught to keep our hands and feet to ourselves.

At amusement parks, this is also a good idea. Keeping your hands and your feet inside the car at all times is not only a smart suggestion, but it guarantees that you'll get to keep those hands and feet after the ride!

As we get older and our spaces become less structured, this affects our personal space. Not everyone is a hugger. You'll know when you go in for a hug and a side-arm block reaches in! Take social cues like that and learn from them.

Think about girls and guys and how they exist in each other's space. What can make you feel uncomfortable? As you and your friends mature (both guys and girls), it'll be increasingly important to respect each other in that process.

If someone is sitting too close or doesn't have a good gauge on personal space, politely let them know that you're not comfortable. This person probably didn't know they were in your space and will be more aware next time. You can lead the way in this.

And if you have a tendency to think that everyone feels as comfortable as you do, ask yourself, "Am I in someone's space in a way that would need their permission?" If you're asking yourself that question, then you probably need to create some distance or ask, "Hey is it cool if I sit next you on the bus?" Or you could say, "Hey I didn't mean to make you feel uncomfortable. I'm a hugger, but high fives are great if you're more comfortable with that."

THOUGHT #95

TALKING NICELY

When you don't know what to say or if you're tempted to say something that doesn't bring life, follow these simple steps.

- Step one: Say something nice.

- Step two: Try not to be rude or showy; just be nice.

- Step three: Look at the person, and listen, if you have time. Nod your head and let them know that you're really listening. Nice!

THOUGHT #96

GIVING DIGNITY

We once read about a man who grew up as a missionary in Africa. In the tribe where he lived, everyone bathed in the same river—including him. Looking back at that situation, he never felt like it was gross, weird, or awkward. As people bathed, other people respected their dignity and preserved it by honoring them without saying harsh things or staring at each other. It was a natural thing for them to be this way—preserving each other's dignity had become a way of life.

When can you give others the decency of dignity? When his voice cracks. When her body changes. When his pants are too short. When something embarrassing happens to her in public. When his friends change but he hasn't. When her world crashes in heartbreak. You will face so many scenarios and opportunities to care for people by preserving their dignity and honor.

Be an architect of hope—no matter who you're with.

WHAT'S DIFFERENT OTHER THAN BODY PARTS?

No one gets all the way to junior high without realizing that there are differences between guys and girls. Sure, there's the biology stuff, but there's much more than that. But most of the non-body differences are more "tendencies" than hard differences, largely because we're all very shaped by how our culture tells us we should act and think.

For instance, girls usually form friendships through talking. But guys usually form friendships by doing things together—even though talking is important to them, too.

Girls are *way* better at understanding and interpreting emotions than guys are. Guys—especially teenage guys—often misread other people's emotions.

And here's a reality that can sometimes feel weird at your age: Girls usually go through puberty (and all the stuff that comes with that, including growing taller and getting an adult-shaped body) a year or two earlier than guys. That's why so many sixth- and seventh-grade girls seem so much taller than their male peers.

God made us all unique. And while there are some differences in the *average* guy and the *average* girl, you are not average—you're one-of-a-kind! So don't feel limited by who people think you should be (because you're a guy or a girl), and don't put other junior highers in a box either.

GUYS TEND TO MISS THE IMAGE OF GOD IN OTHERS

Way back at the beginning of this book, we talked about how one of the most unique and wonderful things about you is that you are made in the image of God. When God was creating everything in the world, he chose to make humans *like him* in some really beautiful ways, including our minds and emotions and ability to choose.

But because of all the messages we receive from our culture (about who we are and how we should behave and the things we should think are important), most of us don't notice the image of God in others and ourselves.

For guys, this usually shows up in the way they think of and look at girls. Guys have been lied to and told that women are something for men to use for their own enjoyment. That view sometimes causes guys to think of girls as "things" rather than people. Guys, if all you notice about a girl is how she looks, you're missing the chance to see something amazing about God.

GIRLS TEND TO MISS THE IMAGE OF GOD IN THEMSELVES

Girls have heard all the same false messages, of course. They've been lied to and told that if they want to get attention or affection — if they want to experience *love* — they have to put themselves on display for guys.

Girls, you know that you are much more wonderful and amazing than a cute toy for guys to notice. But when you go along with those expectations in our culture, you can slowly stop noticing the image of God in your own life.

Don't play that game. The God of the universe lovingly and uniquely made you, and you have within you his own character and strengths.

A Story From Junior High Brooklyn:

Craig is cool. I like him, so I think I'll steal his hat.

{Fast-forward three weeks}

I can't believe my parents let me go to the movie theater with my friends—and Craig. He's sitting next to me, and I'm about to pass out. We end up holding hands and if someone asked me about the movie we just watched, I'd have no idea what it was about. I'm waiting for a few minutes before my ride gets here. I have no idea what's supposed to happen next. I feel like maybe we shouldn't be in this place because I don't know what I would say if there is something more than holding hands involved in all of this. I like him. But does he really like me, too? I think I'll ask my best friend to go to the bathroom with me. That should buy me at least 10 minutes to figure things out. #easyout